Kaleidoscope Views

Short story glimpses of life

By

Mr Fred D. Farris

Kaleidoscope Views

Glimpses of Life
Short story visions of life

By
Fred D. Farris

Acknowledgements

I am grateful for encouragement and help received from fellow members of the Kansas City Writers Group. A special thanks to Deborah Shouse for her cogent critique and generous review on the back cover.

Other valuable help came from my 'Homer's Orphans' critique group and sessions with good writing friends.

I am especially indebted to my wife, Joann, for manuscript proofing, re-typing and computer savvy. And thanks to Denise Farris and Noelle Nauss for the use of their photographs.

* * *

About the Author

Fred Farris sold newspapers on the street in St. Louis at age 12. He slogged through Germany as an infantry sergeant in WWII then graduated from Westminster College. He later led his own advertising agency for 45 years in Kansas City which honed his acumen for writing what advertising practitioners call "Truth, well-told."

He turned to fiction upon retiring at the age of 75.

His short fiction stories have been published widely in Anthologies and Magazines in the Midwest, East Coast and South.

See also Fred's other book, "Bridges of Life," published in 2010 by Digital Press in Kansas City.

Introduction

Kaleidoscope Views presents both fiction stories and essays.

Most of these writings are fiction ... small glimpses of life -- reflecting bits of peoples hopes, challenges and dreams ... visions like the changing images seen through a kaleidoscope ... Tales of human joys and struggles.

* * *

The Short Fiction Story

A view through others eyes ... the thrill of adventure, fear or frolic.. a sudden glimpse or revelation illuminates a small corner of human existence --. The Short Story gives in a page, what could not be revealed in a volume.

The Short Story length is generally up to about 25,000 words. A 'Short Short Story' or "Flash Fiction" is usually about 1000 words or less. All stories must have a beginning, a middle, and an end.

Two Flash Fiction stories presented in these pages, 'Movie Line' and 'Exit Poll' won 1st and 2nd Place Awards in writing contests conducted by the Kansas Authors' Club and the Missouri Writers' Guild.

... Fred Farris

Kaleidoscope Views

Table of Contents

Providence

Donito looked down at the brand new 1972 half-dollar in his hand. President Kennedy's silver image stared up at him, as if to say, 'Onward.' Uncle Jose had given it to him for his tenth birthday and his coming trip to grandmother's house in far off

St. Louis. His dad had gone west to harvest California's ripe melon fields and his mother had died, so Donito must also leave the Arizona ranch. 'Ito' means 'little one'-- rail-thin and knobby-jointed, he looked like he'd been assembled from Tinker-Toys and topped with a black rag-mop. Shy hazel eyes.

Never again would Donito chase jackrabbits with his dog Pepe or unearth fragments of pretty pottery from ancient Zuni Indian villages.

At the bus station in Phoenix, Uncle Jose bought a one-way ticket to St. Louis and handed it to Donito.

"Put it in your pocket, don't lose it. Your bus leaves at 4:30. Watch that big overhead clock."

"Si, si Uncle," Donito stuffed the ticket down in his backpack. He then deposited the half-dollar deep into the pocket of his blue jeans where it jostled a piece of paper with grandmother's phone number in St. Louis. His hand also lingered there to fondle four quarters he had earned cleaning out chicken coops. That dollar-and-a-half made him rich.

Uncle Jose also gave a quarter to the porter wearing a fancy red and black cap.

"Be sure this boy gets on the correct bus to St. Louis; OK?" he told the redcap.

As Uncle Jose chugged away on his motorcycle, Donito waved goodbye. An uncertainty wafted the cool air, a feeling of loss and change.

The Greyhound bus station in Phoenix bustled with travelers. Donito waited near the front of the line of passengers. His mind throbbed with the eagerness of adventure. The arriving bus lumbered into the station -- its engine roar resonated, amplified by the low ceiling. A giant Greyhound dog painted on the bus's side seemed to gasp for breath as the engine growled. It crawled forward, nose close enough to sniff the tortillas in Donito's back pack. The bus door opened and passengers emerged. Some hugged greeters and some walked off alone.

Overhead, a loud-speaker blared, "Departure will be delayed for about an hour for minor engine repair, and the lunch room is now open." Donito unslung his small backpack containing four tortillas, a bottle of water, a plaid shirt, change of underwear and a toothbrush his uncle gave him -- all he had in this world. He sat on a long wood bench in the waiting room. Great adventure lay ahead. He could do it! He was brave. Had he not killed the poisonous scorpion crawling on his baby cousin's crib? Even though small for his age, he faced the bus trip as a whole new world. He felt macho.

The day before, back at his village, Father Estoban had given him a blessing for the long travel adventure.

"*Vaya con Dios*. Go with God. Providence will provide for you," the Padre said, then added, "And remember you are blest with a famous name, 'Little Don,' for Don Quixote He was a gallant knight of old Spain who fought for noble causes on his journey into strange lands just like you will."

The priests moving hand blessed the boy with the sign of the cross, as he added, "Don Quixote was brave and so are you, your long trip will be great fun."

Soon Donito would climb aboard the huge bus. Across the lobby, a lunch counter faced him with a phone booth standing before it. Loud speakers blared again. The loud voice said his bus to St. Louis was being further delayed and wouldn't depart for another forty minutes.

Donito stood up to stretch. He left his backpack on the bench, walked across to the lunch counter, bought a chili hot-dog with 60 cents and went right back to his bench. Before biting into it he fondled the warm bun -- fingers dipping into the chili like taste buds savoring the food before it entered his mouth.

An older boy about fourteen sat near him, across from the phone booth. When a woman left the phone booth, the kid went into the booth and closed the door. Through the glass Donito saw him tear pieces of newspaper into strips and stuff the paper wad up inside the coin return slot. The kid left. People made phone calls. About ten minutes later, the kid re-entered the booth, fished out the paper wad, and coins clinked down into the coin slot. The kid scooped them out and headed into the lunch room.

A lady cuddling a crying baby fitted into a shoulder sling the way Indian mothers do, sat down next to Donito. Her head shawl flowed down to cover the infant even though it was hot. As the baby's squeal quieted down, Donito dozed off. He awoke as the loud speaker squawked ...

...“Bus leaving for Albuquerque, Amarillo, Oklahoma City, Wichita, Kansas City and St. Louis now boarding at gate 2.”

Donito ran to the gate. The ticket taker held out his hand. Donito fumbled in his pocket and pack -- he searched frantically, but the ticket was gone.

“Step aside and search your pockets,” people said, but Donito couldn't find his ticket.

“I can't be responsible,” the bus driver said, and sent the boy to the station master.

Donito's mind flashed danger when he saw the station master dressed in a uniform like a policeman. He'd been told to stay away from police; they had put his uncle in jail. Donito shrunk back and ran out.

His uncle had said, “Things don't always turn out the way they should. You need to be smart like the coyote.”

He circled around the building and re-entered the station where the bus had come in. He watched redcap porters load luggage into two open compartments in the bus's side panels, one for passenger luggage and another for freight; big boxes, golf bags and a bicycle being loaded in.

When the redcap man stepped away to get more luggage, Donito dashed forward, climbed up into the freight compartment and hid behind a big green Army duffel bag and some wooden crates. The redcap shoved a wire cage in. Donito scrunched backwards. The cage housed a brown-spotted dog – face-to-face just inches away. The dog woofed, just like his own Pepe he had left behind. The small cur looked half collie and half coyote. It pointed its ears back, tilted its head up and howled an eerie cry as the compartment doors slammed shut.

Darkness enveloped little Donito. The bus motor roared, but within a few minutes the engine gradually simmered down to a rumbling drone. A weight of darkness lay on his head like a heavy poncho. Donito's eyes widened to try to see. About two hours out, the dark got heavier. It eroded his confidence as the acrid smell of gas fumes stung his nose. A crack of light danced in from beneath the compartment door as it jiggled on its hinges. The dog crawled close to the near edge of his cage and whined. From his backpack, Donito fed the dog bits of tortillas in the sweltering heat.

Giant rubber tires squealed on pavement. A whizz, whizz of cars zoomed by in the opposite direction in sort of swishing rhythm. It must be raining. No sound came from the dog in the dark but a pungent smell of urine. How much farther to go? Minutes seemed like hours. He had to pee. He remembered going to the outhouse and his fear of spiders there, and of falling into the hole and the insects crawling.

After what seemed like hours, the bus stopped to take on passengers. His stomach grumbled. Sweat soaked his frail body like a full immersion baptism. The compartment door opened – Donito scrunched back and froze trying to be a chameleon lizard. Light streamed in shocking his eyes. He squinted. Men removed a box. The dog moaned. It wasn't guttural but more like a barn doors rusty hinges slowly opening in a cry for help. The redcap walked away. Donito crawled out, peed on the ground, and then ran into the station. He put his last 90 cents into the vending machine, scooped out two candy bars, and scurried back into his secret compartment. As he bumped the bicycle wheel, it rotated. A redcap shoved in a wooden crate. Would he notice the turning bike wheel and look closer? Donito's fist tightened. The bus roared again.

Every hour stretched out into infinity.

"Have I been forgotten?" He prayed the prayer his grandmother had taught him, then visualized the Priest's kind face.

"Help Me Father," begging the old bearded man to touch him. His pulse throbbed in his temples. He was not sure they had been touched, for would not Christ's touch be more gentle? Even though he knew the bus was speeding, it seemed like a turtle. On the ground a turtle moves 97 times slower than a motivated black beetle.

After a long time of the engine's loud roar he gradually adjusted to its drone. Now he heard a different noise; Cree-cree -- barely audible -- cree-cree. Yes, he knew it, it was a cricket, the kind like he used to raise as pets in a little screened box. Cree-cree -- the cricket rubbed its hind legs together in a sing song vibrato. Only the male cricket sings.

He ate his last candy bar as the driver's muffled voice said, "Next stop Oklahoma City."

"How much farther," his mind begged.

The perpetual sway and vibration made his stomach queasy -- plus a noxious smell of exhaust fumes permeated his nose. Now another low murmur, the dog whining, "Couldn't you wait to poop?" Donito asked. It stunk.

Cree-cree, came the answer ... cree-cree. The vibrating floor quavered unmercifully. Now a different echo sounded, sort of muffled and sad. It started up in his head. At first mild-mannered doubt slipped into his mind like a spy. It came garbed in a black shroud like grandmother wore at his mother's burial. He felt himself weakening. His confidence evaporated like a drop of dew in the dessert. Once again the giant engine coughed, jerked and screamed forward. But it was the silence of the stops for lunch, at first a welcome relief, soon became a worry of abandonment. After only a few minutes he welcomed the murmur of voices returning to the bus.

What seemed like eons of hours later, the dark and time became one -- their combined weight distended and magnified his misery. Donito kicked his cramped legs back and forth and pushed and pulled the dog's cage back and forth just for exercise. The dog whimpered like a vanquished greyhound racer coming in last.

"I must not give in," Donito said aloud. He thought of the fresh breeze back at the ranch chicken-yard, and watched golden brown hens scratch and cackle in their strangely lyrical talk. He remembered their droppings in their egg laying house-- pure white and odorless compared to dog poop. He longed to see pure white again..

More long hours in the black. He named the dog Pepe ... and the cricket was Jiminy like in "Pinocchio."

"You look like the dog that chased raccoons away from my chicken yard," he said.

"Cree-cree." It was Jiminy who answered -- always the same rhythmic answer.

"Lets go on a bicycle ride," the boy said as he spun it's wheel with his hand.

The bicycle answered, "Pedal fast and let's get outta here."

"*Yip, yip*," the dog said, "Take me with you when you leave."

But Donito knew the end of their friendship would be soon. "Will he forgive me for abandoning him?"

A sudden swerve brought back reality as a cargo box shifted and bumped his bony knee-cap. It hurt. The dark wall of human loneliness made him feel discarded, like a used corn husk thrown to the chickens.

His solitary confinement cramped in closer and closer. Donito pushed his legs against the box again and again to exercise his dormant muscles. Corrosive thoughts ran free-footed in his fertile mind.

"Am I going to die?'

Now the engine's drone, rather than subdued, became louder, pulsing, pounding, assaulting his eardrums. He couldn't sleep.

He wondered if he would starve in St. Louis. "Will I be caught and put in jail?'

Finally ... he heard the bus driver's welcome call.

"All out for St. Louis,"... as the bus chugged into the terminal. He visualized his dash to freedom. Anxious moments drug on. Shards of neon lights flashing through the crack in the door promised liberation.

Hydraulic air brakes discharged a loud discordant exhaust. The squeaking high note of the compartment door opening put the boy in motion. Squinting at the light, he climbed out. He stumbled -- body fluids having been at low ebb -- then recovered and bolted away from the grasping hands of surprised baggage men. Donito circled around and came back into the station's front waiting room. He searched everywhere for grandmother, but she was not there ... and he had no money left to call her number. Puzzled and scared he sat on a bench -- what to do?

But then -- a glorious sight met his eyes. Father Estoban was right. Providence was fulfilled. There, standing like tall statues, were five telephone booths -- his bank vaults lined up in a row like sentinels guarding his new coin slots.

End

PLAYING AT THE GAME FARO

Brother Mark and the Gypsy

Robert sprinted along the dark alley ... "Stop," a voice shouted from behind.   Heavy footsteps splashed on the wet asphalt -- coming closer. Robert's chest pounded.

Raindrops smeared his glasses with a kaleidoscope of distant lights. He stumbled.   Lightning flashed its jagged white teeth in the black night revealing a brick wall beside him. He leaped up, elbows on top of the wall, threw one long leg of his slender body over -- pulled up and landed catlike on all fours on the other side. He crouched, hands in mud -- listening for the footsteps outside the wall. He wiped his hands on the coat-tails of his Brooks Brothers suit and breathed easier as the footsteps faded.

Now a different sound came. Men's voices singing softly, like a muffled Gregorian chant. It came from inside the dimly lighted windows of a two story building with a vaguely medieval appearance. He moved toward it. A carved stone plaque revealed itself in another flash of lightning – 'Christian Brothers Monastery of Boston.' How opportune Robert thought -- he always made his own good fortune.

He humbled himself down for the role, opened the big oak door and slunk in like an actor on the stage.

A brown robed man with beard to match rose from a table and shuffled silently toward him.   Robert slumped his shoulders, bowed his head a little to feign humility.

A gnarled ivory hand extended itself from within the open sleeve of the monk's brown robe.

"Welcome brother, we've got some hot coffee in the kitchen -- my name is Brother Zabata." A faded scar on his jaw stretched as he spoke.

"I'm Robert," he said quietly ... and thought the Monk looked like a sucker he'd duped in a card game last year. What a perfect set up for a hideout.

They joined another brown clad monk in the kitchen cleaning up a still warm oven. After a slice of bread with peanut butter and silence, Brother Zabata said, "Follow me Robert." They shuffled along an outside portico walkway. Cooing pigeons in the arched eaves echoed an eerie murmur. The monk opened a door into a little room with a bed, chair and table lamp. A monk's brown robe hung on the wall.

"Sleep well Robert," the voice under the hood said, "we can talk in the morning if you feel like it. You can use that robe if you need to keep warm."

Four days later, May 20, Robert pondered the time he had wasted in boring meditations in this stone crypt with hooded men. *What Chumps.* They all looked lost and gaunt. Their robes reminded him of tribal leaders in Afghanistan. In the lavatory Robert looked in the mirror with his new hood up over his head ... his Roman nose protruded ... his dark secretive eyes sunken back in his head. He tossed his head back to make the hood fall on his shoulder, washed his face and started to light a cigarette.

"No smoking here," a monk said.

"No problem," he inserted the cigarette behind his ear in a defiant gesture.

At the bare wooden breakfast table, the hot coffee tasted good. Brother Zabata sat down across from him.

"Good morning Brother Zapata," he said, "Is that Spanish?"

"Yes, it means shoe," the monk grinned.

Robert stifled a smirk ... *Just for kicking around*, he thought, as they ate bread in silence.

Three days later Robert sneaked out at night and walked two blocks toward the Boston Common. It hurt his ego as a con man to steal outright, like a lowly thief. He's smarter than that. But now he needed money quickly to pay his past-due apartment rent and get out of that monk mausoleum. He would lower himself to do this one burglary. He remembered his dad's words, "Better to be a starving hound dog than a man without money." He thought back to his father's funeral where the Priest threw a white cloth over the black coffin, waved some gray smoke around it and intoned a chant.

Robert looked for an easy target. An old frosted glass door read Auntie Ems Antiques and Art Shop. Its ancient door-latch invited his eye. He felt in his pocket and withdrew his pearl-handled pocket knife. He slid the knife blade in the old door-jam, heard it click, opened the door and entered. Just inside, he stood still a few seconds adjusting to the dark. A faint florescent glow about ten steps forward cast a shadow on the wall -- it came from an old-fashioned upright cash register on the counter. Behind the counter, on a desktop, someone had left a computer screen on, its soft glow emitted just enough light so he didn't have to use his pocket flash-light. He hesitated -- listened to the silence, then slowly walked to the cash register and pushed the lever to open the cash drawer. It dinged and he lifted out a handful of dollars.

From the corner of his eye, a slender form moved and rose from a sofa in the dim light. It looked like a young girl in a dress – all bluish from the computer glow. She stood up and remained still. Robert's mouth went dry. The last thing he wanted was confrontation.

"Don't worry I won't hurt you, don't scream," he whispered, try-ing to sound reassuring.

She took a step back. "I'll call my Aunt," she threatened.

"Please don't, I'll put the money back, I needed it for my sick mom."

The girl took another step back. He put the dollars back in the cash drawer leaving it open. "See, I'm not a thief, see I'm leaving." He took a step back.

"Wait," she said. "Don't con me," She lifted a dollar from the drawer and handed it to him. "Now get out and don't come back," her voice steady. She was close enough for him to see a hint of shoul-der length dark hair and bluish complexion cast on her face from the computer screen. His worry subsided. He wanted to say, hello, but thought better of it. "Thank you," he said, and walked out quickly.

Maggie sat back down on the sofa in the dim light. Her mind flashed back to her twelfth birthday in 2002 back in Brighton Beach, Brooklyn.

Her mom called her Maglana then. She remembered a new head scarf her mom gave her -- a pretty purple one. She had tied it around her head and cheeks. Maybe it would hide her blemishes from scarlet fever. She looked out her second floor window overlooking Brighton Beach and Coney Island. Their neighborhood, called Little Odessa, had been named for the Ukrainian and Russian émigrés who flooded in about thirty years ago. The Sunday beach crowd just began to spread their beach towels on the sand. A gull swooped low to grab a pizza crust off the boardwalk

Maglana skipped down the creaky stairs and sauntered through her mom's Fortune Telling Parlor furnished with a vinyl covered card table and three folding chairs. Gold and crimson drapery on two walls enhanced its mood of mystery. The aroma of fresh rye bread filtered in from the oven and small bakery in the front room facing the street. She stepped half-way out the front door. The elevated train rumbled overhead.

"Be right back momma, I'm going to the boardwalk," she yelled.

"OK, but take your phone with you and stay away from those guys at the Kiev Restaurant and come back in fifteen minutes."

Good, she didn't want boys looking at her anyway -- especially those tough Russian immigrants who were always fighting Italian Mafia guys for control of the streets, the two cultures clashing like tectonic earthquake plates she had read about in her geography book.

As she closed the front door, a sign on the door, ODESSA BAKERY, written in both English and the Cyrillic alphabet of Gypsies, glowed in red paint.   Since fortune telling was illegal in New York, a list of services next to the bakery sign read:

ASTROLOGY, HOROSCOPE, PALMESTRY
and TAROT CARD READING
By MADAM EDESCU

That evening Maglana sat on the stairs behind the scarlet drapes. She held her computer game-player in her hand. Her mother's voice leaked through the drapes as she talked to an immigrant Russian woman who came in complaining of stomach aches.

"Rub five fifty dollar bills over your stomach, and the bearded man pictured on the green bills, who was a President of the United States, and also a great healing doctor will draw out the devil. Then bring back the cash. I will bury it in a grave -- and your aches will be gone."

People are stupid, her father had told her.

"You're smart, look how good you are with the computer; you'll survive because you put your faith in yourself. Be the hunter, not the rabbit. The rabbit never wins, Greed dominates most people's minds, and they become gullible. Take advantage of their greed, they're suckers."

For her 14th birthday her dad took her to Coney Island Amusement Park. On the way, they browsed through the Russian Book and Gift store where he bought her a little gold cross on a necklace.

On the Ferris Wheel she grabbed his hand as the chair swung free from the platform. The chair lurched backwards swooping them up. A brisk wind swirled her coppery hair made more golden by the sun. They soared toward white clouds billowing out like eggs. Calliope music accompanied their gondola. She loosened her grip on the bar and pointed to a formation of geese. The leader honked an oboe solo as if to say "Onward." Her dad held her hand as the chair stopped on top. They rocked and laughed, "Remember, it's good to be on top. A gypsy even became Mayor of Budapest," he said.

At 17, her mom taught her the "Twenties" game to encourage her self confidence.

The kid behind the counter of the 7-Eleven Store is pimply faced. Maglana flits down the aisles, making sure she is noticed, drifts up to the counter, running her fingers over the display racks of chewing gum.

"You got a favorite?" she asks the young man.

"Favorite gum?"

"Yeah, I don't know which kind to buy – you have an idea?

Pretty girls never asked his opinion. "I like Dentine," he says.

"I love Dentine. "she giggles -- he grins --

"How much?"

"Fifty cents." His voice cracks.

Maglana digs into her pockets, twisting her torso around as she looks for change. The boy tries not to look down her dress at the soft breasts in front of his face.

"No change, all I got's this ... She hands him a twenty-dollar bill.

"I feel dumb giving you a twenty for something that costs fifty cents."

"It's OK." He pops open the register and gives her the $19.50 and tries to touch the skin on her palm as he transfers the money.

"Thanks," she rips open the gum and pops a stick in her mouth. She leans against the counter, her face just two feet away from his. "So you go to school around here?"

"I go to Roosevelt," he stutters.

"Really ... Cool, I had some friends who went there – Hey that's where I know you from. You're on the football team, right?"

"No," he blushes.

Maglana nods her head knowingly. "Shame," she says reaching out, touching his arm. "Arms like these -- well, their loss, right?"

"Right, sure." His breathing falters.

She smiles -- turns to leave, heads for the door. But suddenly she stops, spins around, comes back to the counter. "I found fifty cents," plopping the two quarters on the counter.

She smiles big ..."For the gum." He almost blushes. "Oh, great," he slides her change into the open register.

"Can I get my twenty back?" she asks, leaning forward blinking those golden eyes. He nods, pulls her bill back out and hands it to her. "Listen," he looks down, hesitates, words sticking in his throat, "Maybe sometime ... we could go out or something." There's no answer. He looks up. There won't be an answer. The bell on the front door is tinkling. The girl is gone.

Back home she shows the extra $19.50 to her mom who hugs her and says,

"My Maglana, you'll never starve."

At 18, on her walk home from high school, Maglana always moved to the opposite side of the street from the Kiev Bar. A guy from there had raped her older sister and got away with it. The older women wouldn't talk about it. In that male-dominated culture, womanizing was legendary. Seduction bordering on harassment was rife.

Her girl friends at high school called her Maggie. They talked about the sexual pressure and some discussed escaping when they graduated. Maggie strolled through a small park. The Maple trees made a silent effort to bloom. Today she could almost feel it in her own body, the surge of the sap in the trees upward, up to the bud tips, there to think about pushing out to new life.

The next morning Maggie woke up smiling. The early sun coming through the venetian blinds cast a ladder of hope on the wall.. a good day for climbing new ventures.

* * *

Maggie stepped aboard the Amtrak. The train's sway and rumble echoed music in her ears. Outside the window, old red brick buildings, squalid back yards and green fields flew past. A guy with a mustache smiled at her and said "Hello."
As they debarked in Boston he walked away trailing a wake of intrigue. She remembered her mother's words, "Men come in many colors like light flooding through stained glass windows."She found a job as a waitress. Four months later she got caught playing the Twenties, but fortunately the mark didn't press charges. The judge released her into the custody of a half-way house run by Auntie Em. It was also an antique store gallery.

Auntie Em liked Maggie and let her help run the store's computer. Auntie Em charged outrageous prices. She said some people have so much money, you should charge high prices for paintings and artwork. People don't want cheap stuff on their walls ... they want to brag to their rich friends about how much they paid, the greater the joy for all. It confirmed their wealth.

Maggie was in her element. She re-priced most of the store's stock doubling many price tags. Auntie Em smiled at the business acumen of her new ward and added an extra couple dollars in Friday's pay envelope.

* * *

A boring indifference weighed on Robert as the aroma of coffee lured him to the kitchen.

"Good morning Robert, you've been here nine days now. I notice you've lost your limp, saints be praised." He raised his hands in mock celebration.

"This old guy is pretty savvy," Robert thought

"You're welcome to stay longer," Brother Zabata said, as if deprivation is exciting, "but we give all new men here a new name for entering a new life."

"Oh! ... How about Judas," Robert grinned.

"Your sense of humor will be of great comfort to you," the priest said stoically.

"I'll rename you Brother Mark, for the writer of the second book in the New Testament."

"Good enuf ... I've always wanted to be a writer."

"So now Brother Mark, we'll start you out with a blessing. I know you like to go out at night, so this is your blessing -- May your soul bless the work you do -- go into the dark night protected and renewed."

"Renewed?" Robert asked, "You mean reborn like Jesus?"

"Well aren't we all seeking hope? ... Let us pray for your new life." He bowed his head. Robert also bowed to be polite. *This praying stuff is for suckers.*

The next day the aroma of fresh baked bread lured Robert into the kitchen. A monk welcomed him and showed him how to knead dough for the evening's rolls.

Next morning, Robert shaved and admired his handsome face in the mirror. He replaced his professor looking horn-rimmed glasses with his other pair, aviator style sun glasses with blue lenses like Robert Redford wore in that movie, "The Sting."

Robert walked with a purpose to see that girl again. Two blocks to the Antique Store passed with anticipation. He stepped inside. Maggie stared at him.

"What do you want? I never expected to see you again," she said ... radiant in her skin the color of tawny vanilla. Auburn ringlets molded the curve of her temple.

"I'm just like you, I'm looking for answers," Robert said.

"You're not like me."

"I was hoping we could do something. You want a Boston crème pie down at the corner deli?"

"You've been watching the Hallmark Channel too much --. Life's not like that".

"I'll level with you, I lost big at poker. Could you lend me five bucks?"

"Get a job. I told you, you can't con me."

"I'm getting a new job in telemarketing -- pay you back soon."

"No," she said emphatically, "but I'll share my Coke." She poured some Coke and ice cubes from her glass into another one and handed it to him.

The television screen blared with the Royal Wedding from England.

"The British got it right. A country should have a Queen. Women are smarter than men," she said.

"You'd be a very good monarch," he grinned.

She sucked on an ice cube. It sounded like an aardvark rooting into an ant hill.

"But you need a little more polish before you're crowned." His smile splashed from ear to ear.

"You could be my jester." She cracked a grin just enough to see a little white.

"Take off those dark glasses, have you been drinking," she asked.

'"No, I don't drink." He pocketed the shades.

She turned and starred at him.

"Your eyes look like two blueberries in a pool of mustard," she said.

"You have a glib way of expressing yourself." He shot her a feigned pain look.

"Just kidding, where's your sense of humor?" she added.

"I got a sense of humor."

"I haven't seen it."

"Did you hear about the identical twins who robbed a bank? "

"No."

"After they were caught they finished each others sentences."

"Haa Ha" she exaggerated. "I swear you act like a tonic on me," *that's what mama used to say to dolts like this.*

She studied him out of the corner of her eye. His profile stood out clearly against the window. A clean shaven jaw; a blooming sucker in the rock garden of life she thought.   *I can pick his flowers.*

"I'm being serious now, we could be partners," he said quietly but clearly in his best sincere mode.

"I could never trust you, you're a practiced liar ... telemarketing!" She raised an eyebrow derisively.

"I'm not. I only do it for hard-earned profit, like being in a stage play, like the one I'm writing. A Broadway producer said he'd listen to it. I'll make money."

"I've got to get some money too," she admitted in a confidential tone, adding, "Maybe my horoscope is favorable today." Then she remembered how her mother produced horoscope cards; how when she needed to print up a new batch, she merely switched the copy around on the prediction cards. June or March were transposed with other months at random. Gemini became Capricorn or Taurus. It was all a farce, a burlesque and yet entertaining. In this drab world of harsh reality, a little self-deception is welcome, like the lottery now run by the state rather than the Mafia, and the government joins the charade by calling it gaming not gambling.

"We'd be a good team," Robert interrupted her thought.

She looked him in the eye, raised her finger and touched her nose in a swiping gesture, a signal known by fellow con men world-wide.

"Where'd you learn that?" he asked. She told him about her mother -- the sign given to another Gypsy, to not be recognized as a fellow con, and blow your cover when you're working a mark. He thought, *She'd be a good partner ...a team can work more scams.*

* * *

Two mornings later, Robert lay in bed. Pigeons fluttered under the eves outside the open window. They reminded him of the sudden flush of birds, two years earlier, taking flight in Afghanistan -- after an IED-explosive device shattered his buddy's foot. He couldn't sleep. Damn those pigeons. His thoughts wandered about pulling off a big con and having so much money he would be a corporate CEO and have his signature made into a rubber stamp for authorizing orders to four vice-presidents. He sank back into a coma of emptiness that was his cell.

After evening vespers, Robert donned his robe, stopped in their library and read "The Religions of Man," by Huston Smith.

Brother Zapata came in and sat down.

"I got tired of the silence in my room," Robert said.

"Time spent in isolated contemplation is worth its weight in gold, Brother Mark."

Robert let that pass. He didn't intend to be labeled with that moniker much longer.

"Why is Jesus any better than a Hindu Brahmin I knew in Afghanistan while in the Army?" Robert said sarcastically.

Zabata poured a cup of coffee.

"Jesus and Brahmin both are beyond understanding and whose words we try on, but our attempt to comprehend them makes our brain burst with our limited senses. Both spiritual forces flow within us."

Zapata paused, then added, "You might call it a soul, a divine energy. The soul doesn't die but passes from body to body and reincarnation becomes perfect. Our own soul is like deep well water, always there to quench our thirst if you just draw from the well."

They discussed baptism and being reborn again into a new life.

"You mean like Pygmalion, the mythical stone statue who came to life? ... sort of like Pinocchio," Robert sneered a sardonic half-grin. The priest let the sarcasm pass.

The bell in the tower echoed the air with clangs ... an accusing voice directed at stragglers to mass.

Back in his room Robert thought, *I know what I do isn't right, but I'm a realist. If I put myself at risk that's my business. Zapata looks at me like I was a cadaver at an autopsy, wholly exposed to scrutiny and assigned to hell because I won't let him sprinkle water on my head.*

The next day they talked and studied again. Robert surprised himself by revealing to the priest he'd met an interesting girl. Then embarrassed by the intimacy he normally wouldn't share, he closed his Bible and blurted, "I've tried to absorb this stuff ... but I don't want to become a stoic, lost in my own mind. I want action."

The crow's feet on the priest's eyes turned taut.

"You think you can dine at the 'faith smorgasbord' and help yourself to spoonfuls to your liking," he said.

"Jesus is God -- absolute truth. Trying to explain things to you is like trying to describe a cathedral to a blind man."

Next morning, Robert put on the comfortable brown robe and headed for the kitchen. He had promised to help bake bread. How tedious it was to watch bread rise. But today it seemed strangely creative and smelled good. The oven exuded a warm epiphany – or was it just his stomach growling

That afternoon, he headed out to see Maggie as if magnetized.

She bent over her Smartphone. As he drew near he looked over her shoulder. She shut off the screen.

"Hi Robert, are you going back into telemarketing -- who do you work for?"

"I work for insurance companies, part time."

"What do you sell?"

"I set appointments for insurance salesmen. I can't sell the policy because I'm not licensed."

"Why don't you get licensed" she said. "Can't you go to school for that?"

"I could, but its hard work."

"You're a savvy guy, you could do it."

"Nah, I've got a big con game in mind -- one that'll make us rich, but it takes two people with guts ... you could join me."

"Are you saying we're two birds of a feather?" She said, fluttering her mascara lashes.

"We'd do great together," he replied ignoring her sarcasm. "Then I could relax and write of our great capers, I could do it. William Faulkner said he was a liar by profession and made money doing it."

"You're no William Faulkner," she said.

"I might become a Damon Runyon and write about 'Guys and Dolls' in that vernacular that made gamblers like us into acceptable characters on Broadway."

After a brief struggle with his imagination in which he pictured her being impressed, Robert reached over and placed a little pink

candy conversation heart on her computer keyboard. It read, U R
CUTE. She cracked a grin.

"Give me your hand, I'll tell your fortune," she said.

"Sure why not." He looked forward to her touch
.He laid his hand in hers, stretching the fingers like a starfish.
Her forefinger traced along the lines of his palm. A slight frown
crept across her forehead.

"Do you believe in God?" she asked.

"Yeah, some kind of a god, I'm not sure what kind though."

"The kind who gives you freewill, lets you make your own mis-
takes?" She glanced up at his blue eyes.

"What are you getting at?"

She opened her mouth as if to speak – then instead, dropped his
hand and shook her head.

"Nothing, we'll finish this some other time." She turned her
head away.

* * *

A week later Robert sat at a table with Maggie at her shop. He
taught her to play the card flip game. They practiced the patter of
the con and the tell signal.

Next day, they enter a luncheon bar; waited until two seats
at the corner of the bar were vacated, next to two Harvard sweat
shirts, a boy and a girl. Robert orders two beers and a bag of
pretzels.

Maggie fumbles with a deck of cards, shuffling them
awkwardly.

"Ok Ok. I know I goofed, but I've got it now," Maggie said, a
little louder than louder than necessary.

"Nah forget it, you MIT tech girls think you're so smart,"
Robert said.

The Harvards glance over – Robert winks at them and they
continue looking at the menu.

"No, I figured it out." Maggie cut the deck, folded them back
together and shuffled them. She smiled innocently at the Harvards.
"Watch."

"I don't want to belittle you, but you suck at card tricks and I don't wanna waste my time. Maybe Harvard here could take pity on you." He offered pretzels.

The Harvards grin. They're sucked in now. Sitting at the bar's corner it's almost like sitting at the same table

"Let them eat their lunch," Robert said, "they don't wanna watch a stupid card trick, you won't do it right any way".

Maggie glanced up." Did I ask him, I asked *you*." She nods at Harvard and smiles.

The boy grins, "Sure, we'll watch," like he's in on it, like he knows he's been cued. This is how it should go down, Robert thinks. This is cool, the sucker's bitten.

Robert grins slightly, "Thanks guys, take pity on her ... you'all married?"

"Nah, just hangin out."

"That's great -- I'm Joe -- what's yours?"

"Glen ... this is Betty." They shake.

Robert turns his grin toward Maggie. "This is Annette the card fumbler." They all nod. Maggie finishes shuffling the cards, fumbling a few on to the bar. She picks them up sticks them back in the pack; fans them out toward Harvard, saying, "Pick a card my educated friend, any card. Don't let me see it - show it to your friend."

"Have another drink -- you'll want it when you screw this up again?"

Maggie ignores Robert, shoots a hurt look toward their new friends as she extends the spread toward Glen. He reaches over and takes one as she turns her head completely away.

Glen shows it to his girl and Robert -- the five of hearts.

"Put it back anywhere you want."

Glen slides it back in the deck. Now Maggie hands the deck to Glen. "Shuffle them as you want." He does and hands it back. They all smile. This is fun.

Maggie starts turning the cards over one by one face up on the bar.

"Gonna get it right," she mumbles, jack, king, six, eight -- flopping on the bar.

"Got this trick from my old aunt who reads tea leaves."

"You ain't done it yet," Robert said.

She flops several more. Then, there it is, the red five of hearts.
They all see it. Robert curls his lip ever so slightly -- just a twinge
like they practiced. Maggie keeps turning cards over.

"Gonna get it right," she continues as smirks are exchanged
among the watchers.

Betty enters in the fun –

"I don't believe you've got an aunt."

Robert nods at Glen, "She's a keeper." They smile as Maggie
flops a few more and stops. She taps the top of the next card.
"Got it this time."

"You ain't got nuthin' -- blew it again." Robert smiles at the
Harvards. They grin back.

"No I've got it right, what do you wanna bet the next card I
turn over will be   Glen's card?"

"What like, like a real bet," Robert replies.

"Yes, a real money bet."

"Get her, I'm giving her a chance to walk away with her head up
and she wants to lose her daddy's money -- these spoiled rich kids."
He shrugs. Robert reaches into his pocket, pulls out two twenties
and throws them on the bar next to the cards.

Maggie turns to Glen – tapping the top of the deck.

"How about you Harvard, how much you and Goldilocks there
bet the next card I turn over is the one you chose?" Glen looks
at Betty, they both glance down to make sure the five of hearts is
there, face up, already dealt ... easy money, no way to lose to this
MIT braggart.

"Bout a thousand bucks," Glen snickers.

"No, I'm serious," she says. "How much?"

Glen looks at Betty; they both grin and fumble with their
wallets.

"Ninety two bucks, that's all we've got on us."

"Put it up." They toss it on the bar.

"Fair enough," Maggie said, adding, "We just bet the next card
I flip over will be the card you picked -- right? Don't want any
misunderstanding."

"Right," says Glen. His eyes say easy money – He'd show this
MIT gal.

No flourish, no fancy motion -- Maggie holds the deck. But reaches down with her other hand to the bar and flips over the discarded 5 of hearts on the bar face down.

Glen is speechless. She scoops the money off the bar, says "thanks for lunch" as she walks off.

Back at Aunties Antique store, Robert said, "You done alright kid, picked up my tell-signal real good."

During the next weeks, they did other con games ... and accumulated $3,000.

The next night, at Maggie's, Robert put his arm around her shoulder. She moved away. He tried a joke.

"I was watching the Boston marathon and saw one runner dressed as a chicken and another as an egg ... and I thought, now who's going to come in first."

"You're improving," Maggie said. *What a dolt ... but he can be my ticket out of here and he's kinda cute.*

Two weeks later, he taught her the "Jamaican Switch," a big time con where you switch a briefcase full of fake US dollars for one with real English Pounds. It's dangerous and requires split second timing before the mark gets wise. They practiced it three times.

* * *

The police sergeant came through the big oak monastery door without knocking.

"Welcome sergeant, what can I do for you?" Brother Zabata asked.

"Just checking the neighborhood, we never caught that guy we were chasing a while back." The cop shifted his gaze to Robert.

"You're new here. You got ID?"

"We, we don't have pockets," Robert stammered.

Zabata interjected. "His name is Brother Mark, he's OK."

Robert worried about the bag under his bed with $3,000 in it, all his and Maggie's stash. The next day he gave it to her to hide in her shop.

* * *

Robert moped into breakfast ... a dejected look in his eyes.

"My girl friend has run away," Robert mumbled to Brother Zapata.

"Oh, what's her name?"

"Maggie."

"I think I know her. She was a ward at Auntie Em's half-way house and attended mass here every Sunday."

Robert felt a slight twinge. *She went to Church??* A new understanding of her, and now she was gone.

"You sure re-named me right," Robert said.

"How so?"

"A Mark is what we call a sucker. I'm the biggest Mark of all. I loved her."

* * *

Robert sauntered along the Charles Riverbank walkway, the path he and Maggie had strolled together. He conjured up her image in a shimmering moon path across the water. He had taken her hand and gently squeezed it.

Here was a life partner, he thought.

She squeezed back and said, "You know *we*'ve got to get out of this business."

Back at the monastery, Robert joined in making breakfast. The bacon in the skillet curled like Maggie's auburn hair and even smelled like her perfume. He retreated to his room and tried writing the start of his stage-play for the fifteenth time. The keys on the typewriter stared back at him like big round eyeballs. Her eyes, warm, fiery.

How he missed her. He vibrated with instinct. He must find her. Together they could help each other survive.

Robert put on his navy blue business suit and his sincere striped tie and boarded the train to New York. At Grand Central Station he transferred to the elevated train to Brighton Beach. A Brooklyn precinct cop on a bicycle glided along the boardwalk. Robert stopped at a booth and bought a New York Hot Dog. Energized by the spicy mustard or maybe the surging throng, he munched along.

Then, there it was -- the Odessa Bakery. Maggie's mothers house, just as she had described it.

Robert stepped inside. Graying auburn hair flicked out from under a blue beret similar to Maggie's. The woman glanced up from wrapping bread loaves. Her jaw line was Maggie's. She looked at his fancy dude suit ... sizing him up.

.   "My name is Robert Peterson and I m looking for Maglana, is she here, I'm her friend," he declared.

A bearded Rasputin, paying for bread at the cash register frowned at him. The sale rang up, and the man glanced back as he walked out.

"Why do you want to see her?" the woman said.

"Because there is a grace about her and I love her."

She stared at him like an owl measuring the distance to its prey. "Come into my office."

He followed her into a gaudy gold and red draped room. They sat at the round fortune telling table.

"Show me your hands." He put them palms up on the table-top. She spread out his fingers.

"These are not the hands of a working man. Do you have a job? What do you do?" Her dark Gypsy eyes penetrated his.

"I'm a telemarketer but I'm going to be a successful writer."

"That logic is about a weak as boiling the shadow of a chicken to make chicken soup."

"Maybe I'll become a baker. I know how to knead dough."

She stood up. "Maglana's not here. When you find her, tell her to call home or better yet bring her back and I'll make a real baker outta you."

Her dark amber eyes flashed. He felt a warm glow like the wires of a toaster turning orange. They were Maggie's eyes.

Outside the bakery door a gray cat skittered across the street disappearing under a black Buick parked next to a sputtering orange neon sign. Robert could only see the two men vaguely. They were no more than one muscled arm on the driver's side, two pair of sunglasses and two billed caps. The Buick's back door opened. A Neanderthal stepped out blocking his path.

'Get in," he ordered, teeth like rotted logs. A tattoo of an AK47 machine gun flaunted his forearm. Robert's pulse raced.

"Where are we going?" he asked. A silent answer came like a cemetery at night.

They drove a block inland and slowed to enter the garage door of an old brick warehouse. Wooden crates printed with Russian stencils stacked shoulder high crept past outside the car. One open crate exposed bottles of Sobreski Vodka. Two crates lay broken open on the concrete floor.

The rear passenger door opened and a bulky man slid in beside him. The man's coat gaped open revealing the blue gun-metal glint in his shoulder holster.

A smell of Vicks Vapor-Rub replaced the sour vodka. The man blew his nose, coughed, turned steely eyes on Robert.

"Where is Maglana? Don't lie to me. I'm her Godfather."

Robert told him about the half-way house – her mysterious disappearance. Then blurted, "I love her, she wasn't running from me. I don't know why." This was not a man to lie to.

The Godfather's black pupils burned into his. Robert's hand trembled as he waited.

"I don't want Maglana abused by those Boston bastards."
He handed Robert his business card.

"Here's my cell-phone number. Let me know if you find her."

He handed Robert a hundred dollar bill.

"Take him to Grand Central Station," he commanded the driver.

Three months later, Robert had searched for Maggie all over town. Auntie Em said she left no forwarding address. The next day he stepped into a 7-Eleven Store. Robert stared past the mascara of the girl clerk and centered his gaze on a near naked woman on the cover of Penthouse Magazine. He averted his eyes to glance out of the store-front window. And there Maggie was walking down the street, coming toward the 7 Eleven.

Almost intoxicated by the discovery, he rushed out the door just as she approached.

Their eyes met. A frown filtered her face. She brushed her finger on her nose, their signal of not wanting contact right now.

He obliged ... walked on by several steps and turned around. She entered a restaurant and sat at a table with two men. A well dressed portly guy and a mustached dude. He recognized the guy, a loan shark – dangerous to partner with.

In a sudden realization that he needed help from someone he could trust, Robert phoned Brother Zabata on his cell phone.

"I've found her, please help me, I need you."

Robert watched the three plotters order drinks and talk. Ten minutes passed. Then Maggie did the Jamaican Switch of brief cases with a fat guy in the banker's suit. She picked up the brown brief-case he had brought in, and disappeared out a side door. The switch had been made. Maggie and the dude came out of the front door. She carried the brown brief case.

The mustached man followed her closely. They stopped at the rear of a maroon Cadillac. He opened the trunk. She put the briefcase in the trunk. She opened the case and extracted handfuls of currency and started stuffing them into her purse as her share of the take.

Now the man reached out – tried to slam the briefcase shut. She jerked it away.

He slapped her – then hit her arm as they struggled. He slammed the trunk door on her hand. She held onto the briefcase handle. He flashed a knife. He stabbed her. She wouldn't let go. Robert's brain absorbed the nightmarish scene. He lunged toward them. The guy stabbed her again in the arm and throat. She sank to the ground. It was all so fast.

Robert threw himself at her attacker. He tried to pull her away from the thick fingers squeezing her throat.

Maggie on the ground, bleeding, blood flowing from her open throated blouse. Her head flopped backwards.

.The attacker backed off and sped away in the car with the briefcase. Her eyes opened.

"Robert, Robert help me."

"I'm here Maggie." Her breathing tortured. Blood running from her throat.

A police siren sounded in the distance. Her clenched fist clung to a clump of red-stained hundred dollar bills. Her blood running through his fingers, Maggie's warm blood – like being baptized with her blood. She clutched a gold cross around her neck.

"Forgive us our trespasses," she mumbled.

Robert was stunned. How could he have misinterpreted the depth of her real feelings? She passed out; Robert cradled her in his arms.

Brother Zabata arrived − crouched down − sirens getting closer.

Robert blurted, "I want to pray − what do I say?"

"We'll pray later," the Monk felt her pulse.

Maggie opened her eyes. Robert squeezed her hand. She squeezed back.

"Don't let the cops get me Robert," she pleaded, blood flowing from the wounds soaking her blouse.

"We'll take her to our infirmary." Zabata said looking up at the gawkers gathering around. They lifted Maggie to her feet. She slumped, put an arm around Robert's neck.

As they limped off, Robert turned his head to people gathered around.

"I'm her Brother Mark, she'll be alright now," a glint flashed in his brain, *it's the first time I've used that name.*

* * *

. .A bright September sun warmed down on Brighton Beach. The crowded Labor Day crush of people frolicked and fumbled. Kids of all ages stepped into frothing surf ... plunging, floundering, seeking sandy bottom.

Madam Edescu cracked a thin grin as she sat at her computer and read her Email again for the third time.

Dear Mom. I'm coming home ... and .bringing a new baker's apprentice with me.

End

Whether a kaleidoscope view is limited or long, it's always hopeful.

Never denying, but assuring ... like a fruit salad.

The next story,"*Movie Line*" won Second Prize in the Missouri Writers' Guild Contest in 2010 for Short-Short Stories of 100 words or less.

A short-short story must have a beginning, a middle and an end.

Movie Line

She stood in the concession line in the cinema lobby. She ordered popcorn and paused at the butter dispenser. His eyes met hers and lingered a second. She cracked a thin smile. Butter the color of her hair poured on her popcorn. She appeared to be by herself. She turned toward the theater entrance to see the 007 spy movie.

He must act fast.

He extended his hand and flashed his sincere smile.

"Bond, James Bond", he said.

She grinned, shook his hand and replied,

"Lost, get lost".

End

Catfish Voodoo

"I'll give you 75 cents for the whole batch of 'em," Mr. George, the balding storekeeper sneered, looking down at Frank's faded blue jeans torn at the knees.

Frank bit his lower lip... a full day's catch of catfish and carp from the bayou lay in his hand-cart; almost 25 pounds. Frank searched the storekeeper's gaunt face, eyes oddly sunk almost like they were scared of the light.

"Is that the most you can do Mr. George, that's only three cents a pound?"

It was 1940 and most working men, and boys like Frank, if they were lucky enough to have a job, made only two dollars a day in the bayou parishes of Cajun Louisiana.

"If you were a member of our Brotherhood you'd get an extra five percent bonus for all your fish", the storekeeper said.

"Brotherhood?" Frank raised a black eyebrow. .

"Yeah, we help each other find guidance through business and spiritual help."

"Spiritual help? You mean it's a kind of a church?"

The store owner grinned. "Yes, we're called Wiccans. We meet here at the store on Saturday nights."

"Do you do weddings in your church?"

"Sure, we call them Handfastings. The bride and groom hold hands tied together with colorful ribbons. It's a lovely ceremony with vows to each other and to our ways."

"Oh?"... Frank waited.

"Tell you what," the storekeeper added, "I'll give you a dollar and a half for this batch; that's an extra quarter, and you think about coming to one of our meetings. You'd like the folks there."

"Well, I'll think about it, but I ain't saying I'll come for sure."

Frank pocketed the money. Right now he needed money for Maria.

He thought of the first time he saw Maria. She slept in the bottom of his cousin's rowboat. She opened her eyes when he spoke to her and Frank swore two brown doves flew out. She smiled. He knew then that he had to see her again.

A carpet of pine needles crunched under Frank's thin sandals as he turned away from town toward the bayou. A thorn of shame pricked him when the women pointed at him, when they talked of Maria behind her back.

Pausing at the white wooden church, he hesitated, bowed his head then stepped inside. Old Father Budeaux entered the confessional booth as if reading Frank's mind.

"Bless me Father for I have sinned," Frank began.

Through the thin porous screen, he saw the priest rest his chin against his fist like the famous statue "The Thinker." The back of the priest's ancient hand ran rivers of blue through its spotted skin.

He won't understand, he's too old, Frank thought. His tongue felt useless. Then an almost holy aura gave him courage. "Maria's going to have a baby. Will you marry us Father?"

The moment the priest answered, Frank crossed himself and bolted from the church like a racer.He ran past the sawmill where he'd worked last summer. An earsplitting whine screamed as a whirling saw-blade sliced through a pine log. He'd heard that same whine, mixed with his own scream a year ago when that saw-blade sliced off two fingers of his left hand. He cringed as he again saw his two severed fingers drop in the sawdust like two small sausages oozing red. It had taken months of re-learning to use his remaining thumb and forefingers to grip the thick oar of his boat with his claw-like hand. His cousins even nicknamed him 'Claw'.

Frank ran alongside an old freight car, now abandoned by the railroad on one of the side tracks. His Cousin Bobby's family lived in the rusting boxcar now. "What's your hurry Claw," Bobby yelled. He didn't mind the nickname, It was better than François, his real one.

Frank flashed a grin and a quick wave. He angled to his right on a dirt lane under a canopy of Cypress branches and headed toward a small frame house next to the bayou.

Maria opened the torn screen door and stepped out even before he knocked. Her tawny pupils made little stars. He extended his damaged hand up and cradled her chin between his thumb and forefinger. Maria kissed its scars and looked up into his eyes.

"Father Budeaux said yes," he blurted.

Maria burst into tears. "I love you Frankie." Her praline sweet voice always went into his heart; his gut. Now they'd have a proper wedding in church. No more public shame. Maria's cousins would be both jealous and happy.

"It will be a boy," Frank bragged, "and I'll teach him how to fish." He lifted her small left hand to his lips and kissed Maria's naked ring finger.

"I'll put a real gold wedding ring on this finger."

"Wonderful, then I'll be Mrs. Frank Landrey." Her auburn hair bounced as she jumped up and down. Most of Maria's cousins didn't have wedding rings these days. Some borrowed their mother's ring, if she had one, then gave it back.

Hand in hand Frank and Maria watched a blue heron step his long legs over to a new fishing spot. A lone loon added an oboe solo. An amber sun slipped below the bayou horizon.

The bayou used to offer up more of a living for a man willing to troll her day and night. This year, however, a marine blight invaded local water. Some called it a voodoo curse. Fish were dying. Most survivors were smaller than the fat twenty-pounders common in years past, and now Frank needed money for their engagement party. It would be the customary pig roast so neighbors would see Frank could provide for his new family.

He also needed money for Maria's ring he had promised.

"Let's get married next Sunday," Maria cooed.

"Good, then we'll have the pig roast on Saturday."

Frank fished from dawn to dusk every day, still he only had enough money for the pig roast ... not for the ring.

Cousin Bobby arrived early on Saturday. "Let's chop more logs, we need a really big fire, it's got to burn all day," Bobby said.

The two men piled pine logs as high as their belt buckles. They prepared a seventy-pound porker, struggling to clamp the whole pig between two metal farm gates like one giant pork sandwich. Two more neighbors helped lift and hang the hulk beneath iron poles forming a tent-like frame. Then the four master chefs maneuvered the heavy pig-rig over the log pile.

Mr. George chugged to a stop in his black Model-A Ford and stepped out.

"I see you're going to have a Balefire," the storekeeper said, looking at the rig.

"It's a fire for our pig roast, our wedding party," Frank said.

"Have you thought any more about having a Wiccan wedding?" the storekeeper asked.

"Thanks, but Father Budeaux's going to marry us."

"Oh?" ... The storekeeper's eyes seemed darker, ominous, like a jilted suitor. He stomped back to his car and sped away trailing dust.

"Watch out for that guy," Bobby warned, "I went to a couple of their meetings, they're witches ya know, and he was making a Qureant."

"A what?" Frank asked.

"A Qureant, they're questions they ask about you before casting a spell, and a Balefire is their fire ritual."

Frank remembered old talk about some strange pagan rituals when he was a kid. The tales had spread like kudzu-vine through the bayou.

"What a bunch of crap," Frank said, "But don't tell Maria, she'll worry."

They lit the fire before noon, so by dusk, glowing coals shimmered upward, enveloping and simmering the charring pork. Each quarter-hour two guys rotated the metal gate clamping the pig to a new position. All afternoon neighbors came by to slap Frank on the back and slather the pig with long handled brushes dripping with spicy-sweet vinegar and Creole red pepper sauce. Pork fat and sauce dripping on the fire sizzled, crackled and smoked the roasting dinner all day long.

An hour before sundown people began arriving. The smells of barbecue smoke, burnt wood and charred pig-skin floated over the twilight.

Father Budeaux pronounced it all, "An ethereal essence."

Cajun chef friends with freshly sharpened Bowie knives sliced deep through the skin to cut slices from the pig's burnt blackened ribs. Crispy barbeque, skin and-all, scorched eager fingers. Sorghum molasses on golden cornbread yielded tastes of heaven. Other neighbors brought crawfish jambalaya with tasty "dirty-rice dressing" and homemade rice beer.

Father Budeaux removed his collar, loaded his plate again and proclaimed, "No greater pleasure upon the palate of man."

Maria, in her orange skirt made from cloth of dyed chicken-feed bags, swirled as she danced ... never seeming to tire.

A jews harp's nimble twang harmonized with a happy harmonica. A frisky fiddle and French concertina blended folk-tunes, ragtime and country blues in a Cajun cadence. Serpentine melodies curled around dancers' feet. Girls flirted then looked away. Boys nodded and smiled, not looking away. Passionate chords entered their veins like the sizzling meal. Frank and Maria rocked to the rolling rhythm, and the beat came from their pounding hearts.

Grandmas and grandpas stomped in circles with little kids. Teenagers two-stepped until well after dark as their shadows flickered on and off pine trees. By ten o'clock, most everyone had sauntered toward home.

Frank drew Maria aside. "I'm going to fish all night to get more money for your ring."

"Be careful," she pleaded, with a long moist kiss.

Leaving Maria with his trusted friend Bobby, Frank headed for his rowboat. The water close in front looked like black silk with tiny silver ripples. Frank drove the wide oars into its darkness as the prow parted the water on a final mission before the next day's wedding.

A night loon moaned. A dead fish scale glinted on the bayou from the moonlight. In the moon-bright, a black shadow of a muskrat slinked along the shore; a robber on the run. The muskrat reminded Frank of the storekeeper who a couple weeks ago had shown him a tray of gold rings and crucifixes kept in a carefully locked case.

"I can pay you half down today for a ring and give you the rest in a couple weeks," Frank had offered, but the greedy man countered, "Leave me your boat as collateral."

However wouldn't that be like hocking his soul to the devil? His boat; his father's boat before him, was the one thing of value Frank owned in this world. A man with a boat can promise a woman she will have food for the table.

Frank hung a coal-oil lamp over the boat's side hoping the light would lure fish. He always mouthed "Thankee Lord" when he landed a big one. Tonight he hoped more than ever for a big one.

In the moonlight he struggled to bait his hook with a crawdad.

The whish of his fishing line whipped forward. Its sound reminded Frank of his French grandfather's tale about the lash of a whip cracking over bare-backed workers on a Martinique sugar plantation a hundred years ago. The repeated whish ... whish caught at his soul as Frank cast out into the dark. It also made him think of old voodoo curses some folks still believed, even to this day about this bayou; the story about a young girl disappearing and the one about a midnight murderer.

The dank dark covered Frank's head like a damp veil.

A mildew odor crept out of the mist reminding him of things better forgotten.

A full moon beamed through an opening between the dark clouds. It cast dark shadows from overhanging tree branches onto the water. Shadowy lines on the water transformed into the snake-whip his grandfather had described. *I'm not going to let that mumbo-jumbo of the storekeeper poison my mind.* With a flick of his expert arm Phillip plopped a crawdad into the center of the watery apparition, shattering it into shards.

A soft splash of an oar dipping in the water came from his left ... or wait! Was it behind? ... There it was again or was it his imagination? Who else would be out on the bayou at night? ... Especially this dark night.

"Don't think about it," he told the night. Just think about my wedding to Maria tomorrow.

Only a few small fish fell for the lantern's lure. A dreary dawn hung silent gloom over Frank's meager catch.

Early sun fingered through trees revealing myriad flecks of plankton in the deep prism of the water. A fat water spider skimmed along the surface; choice bait for carp. Frank grabbed into the water, closing his fingers around the spider. A stabbing

needle prick of pain burned his wrist. An olive-green water moc-
casin, the size of a fat water hose, slithered away. Pencil-thin snake
babies wiggled behind their mother, disturbed from their nest.

Two fang punctures showed on his wrist.   He must stop the
venom from going up the arm toward his heart. With his knife, he
cut an "X" slit into each fang mark. He sucked his wrist and spit.
A purple swelling rose but fortunately didn't inch up his arm. He
sucked and spit again. Frank grabbed the bandana off his head and
made a tourniquet around his arm above the bite.

Don't panic .. Nausea made him light headed. *I can't pass out.
What would happen to Maria and the baby?*

Reaching into the water Frank gathered swamp weed, made a
poultice and put it on the purple welt ... at least it wasn't spreading
up his vein.

A swamp owl screeched close overhead, but its normal hoot was
barely audible. Frank slapped his head with his hand ... was he slip-
ping? He remembered when his father had been snake bitten and
claimed the venom in his blood would be passed on and give his
son some immunity to the poison.   He gulped more water from his
canteen and the nausea subsided. He sucked on the wound and spit
again and again.

A high noon sun burned his face. He splashed cool lagoon water
on his face and arm. Thank God the purple was not spreading up
his arm. "Thank you Dad," he mumbled as he ate his cheese sandwich and gradually felt better.

Now there was only one alternative left. One he dreaded.
Cousin Bobby had suggested it, but Frank rejected the idea of
hand-fishing, called Noodling, for giant catfish. Bobby had almost
drowned last year in a Hand–Fishing contest for a big $10 prize.
Noodling was a dangerous sport. You dive into the water and hand
wrestle a monster catfish deep in his own home habitat. Guys had
drowned in those competitive contests before. A giant cat could
weigh 100 pounds or more, have sharp spikes on its upper spine and
fight like the devil. You should have a partner nearby just in case.

There was a deep hollow just round the bend ahead where giant
catfish had been known to spawn. Frank pulled the oars through
the thick water as if drawn by a magnet.   Sweat trickled down his
back. He coasted toward a fallen cypress trunk, half submerged

-- ideal cover for big catfish breeding. His mind said, *No, it's dangerous and I'm tired.* But time was running out.

He tossed the anchor rope over a rotting Cypress trunk protruding from the water -- put two legs over the side and stared down into the olive green depth. A vague apparition stirred four feet down, then took shape -- a big one, the color of tarnished silver hovered. He hesitated in a flash of fear ... then eased over the side, slowly sliding into the water. Stealth was needed here.

He took in a deep breath and submerged. His bare feet oozed into the muddy bottom displacing a crab. Opening his eyes, cool water pressed in and blurred onion greenish. He stared ahead. There -- he couldn't believe it -- right there, under the sunken tree limb, an arm's reach away, a giant ugly catfish hovered. Its long feeler whiskers spiked out around an open bucket-size mouth baring its teeth. Its round eyes stared at him like he was a crayfish hors d'oeuvre. He thrust his left hand forward into its gaping toothy mouth. Blood oozed from his hand staining the greenish water with pink streaks like Easter egg dye. The giant fish twisted its huge scaly body, almost as big as his own. It thrashed violently back and forth to escape.

In another quick thrust, Frank circled his other arm around the slippery body and plunged his clawed right hand into the monsters pectoral gill.

He squeezed his grip with both hands, inside and out, of its slippery body. He held on tight. It bucked like a bronco, its scales scratching his chest. He lost his footing, stumbled to upright himself in the slippery bottom. He wrestled the giant upward, but couldn't get his own head above water. The great tail slashed like a scythe blade against his knees forcing him off-balance.

It seemed like he'd been under at least a minute. His lungs about burst, he struggled to hold on -- slipped in the mud and lost his footing again. Now, finally thrusting his head up above water and gasped. The monster's added weight sunk his bare foot down in the mud.

The huge fish flailed and twisted violently. He pulled its silver-purple head up above the surface -- and boosted the thrashing body half way out. But now its true out-of-the-water-weight overwhelmed his strength. He couldn't hoist it high enough to get it up over the gunwale into the boat. He squeezed the wiggling giant to his chest harder.   He sucked his foot out of the mud then lost his footing again. He struggled slowly toward shore. The monster's weight escalated with each stumbling step. He finally wrestled it up onto land and collapsed on top of his still flailing prize. He heard the sound of its scales still thrashing the ground beneath them.

Exhausted and bloodied, Frank laid on top the fat carcass. His chest heaved for a full minute against the giant until it stopped wiggling. He rolled off. The sun reflected off its lavender patina body. It even smelled good. He whispered, "Thankee Lord."

Frank dragged his treasure through the storekeeper's front door and onto the weighing platform. A dock hand helped lift and hang it on the weighing scales hook. It dangled by its gill magnificently. The sun cast its giant shadow on the wall. People stared at it.   The needle quivered and stopped at 91 pounds for the big catfish alone, plus some little ones totaled 106 pounds.

Mr. George stared at the giant fish and shifted his gaze down to the shredded blood- smeared T-shirt clinging off the boy's skinny frame. A thin grin cracked his craggy face -- the biggest prize cat-fish he'd seen for many months.

He reached down into his display case and lifted the tray of gleaming yellow gold wedding rings up on the counter.

"Take your choice Frank, Maria will be waiting."

End

Aurora Borealis

We strolled silently. I looked up at the sky in awe from my high Colorado plateau.   That inverted bowl we call the heavens flashed ten thousand pinpoints of light. So vast an array and me so small, like a tiny ink spot on the book of life. Just a kibitzer-- a poor player who struts and strains through the pages before the book is closed.

Just then, the Aurora Borealis erupted. A cornucopia of glowing neon rays pierced the sky. Curved streaks of fluorescent greens like layers of mint Oreo cookies exploded, quavered and vibrated the northern heavens. Shifting purple tapestries waved in a wash against a backdrop of star studded dark blue curtains. Silent night, all is bright.

My granddaughter Claire, age12, squeezed my hand, pointed and yelled,

"Look grandpa, isn't that fantabulous?"

She let go my hand, and grabbed her cell-phone-camera-computer-E-book. Her fingers maneuvered down the magic keys. She captured pictures of heaven's beauty as her miracle machine also burst into rock and roll.

A new book opened. If I were a Carillon I'd be clanging.

Who was it who said, "God's in his heaven – all's right with the world?"

Northern lights, holy lights, all is calm, all is bright.

There is no ending to my stroll ...

... I'll just meander down the scroll.

End

Albatross

He watched as she walked to the balcony. Her white silk gown flowing behind her, pressed against her thin fragile form. Head up, proudly leaning into the wind she resembled one of those carved female figures on the bow sprit of an old sailing ship.

Now he said good bye to her and his children. He closed the ancient book he'd been reading; Samuel Coleridge's, 'The Rime of the Ancient Mariner'.

But now it was time, the year was 2354 A.D.

Lee Chainga removed his high mandarin collared jacket and donned the blue uniform of a Captain in the Chinese Navy. He headed out the door toward the Shanghai naval base, trodding over yellow dandelions pushing their persistent heads out of black asphalt bomb craters. At long last, the Admiralty had finally ordered 'Operation Mischief Reef' to be put into action. Captain Chainga remembered his grandfather's dying charge, "Cling to the sea and wait; let nothing beguile it away from you".

The Captain commanded an old light cruiser which had been converted into a submarine rescue ship. His crew of 280 men and equipment and scientists included a helicopter on deck and a deep water submergence vehicle. But its main cargo was a battery of instruments for detecting and measuring radio activity in both air and water.

Their mission would plunge them into danger far out in the South China Sea – waters not traveled by any human for the last one hundred and five years.

"Lets get underway," the captain ordered.

The skeleton outlines of bombed out Shanghai buildings faded into the churning mist kicked up by the ship's propeller. A mustard colored sun behind the skyscrapers whispered farewell.

They passed a channel buoy marker swinging frantically back and forth as if trying to free itself from some giant underwater octopus. Its bell tolled in time with the waves like funeral chimes as the spray flew as vile as sea-monster spit. The captain jammed his hands in his pockets, hunched his shoulders up around his neck and crossed unsteadily over to the starboard side. They set course toward the Philippines whose waters had tested too dangerous with radiation until recently.

Nine days later, the Captain smiled up at a wide-winged Albatross soaring overhead, the seaman's omen of good luck and survival. He recalled an old seaman's tale about a sailor who shot an Albatross and was forced to wear it around his neck as penance for killing it.

Now the big bird's presence, gliding overhead was a welcome sign that dangerous radio-activity levels had finally diminished somewhat. Good news indeed.

He squinted toward the horizon. There, just a blip in the haze lay Mischief Reef. It had been aptly named - only a rogue volcanic crest-- one of a dozen atolls rearing their rocky heads above the lapping waves in the South China Sea off the Philippine coast.

Mischief Reef clung uneasily to its thin sandy surface. A concrete dock loomed. As they drew near, the scene gradually took shape. An old Chinese submarine lay embedded - clinging to the atoll's ridge like a barnacle. It had been washed up on shore in the nuclear holocaust. Its hatch gapped open on its twisted deck.

From under the curved steel hull, jutting rearward, a rusted propeller-blade dug in the sand like a misguided sea urchin.

But the submarine wasn't alone. Jammed in, leaning aft, half on top of the sub was an ancient fishing trawler of old barque design. Its wood structure and single mast were surprisingly preserved and added to the surreal scene.   Captain Chainga knew this island was where World War III had started. Zealots had screamed, "God is great, and he's on my side," at each other until God rebelled.

Beijing had said, "We need the fish from our own rightful waters to feed our people." Washington responded, "International waters must remain accessible." In either case it was about fish.

The insanity at Mischief Reef had erupted when a Chinese submarine in repair dock there, blew up -- torpedoed by a US submarine or underwater drone missile, at least that's what historians said. Most records had been destroyed in the ensuing nuclear exchange long ago. Now, after all these years, this region's air and water had finally tested safe from radiation fall-out contamination.

The Captain wrote a note to his wife in his diary.

"There is a clean fair breeze on this voyage ... Thank God. It's as welcome as your breath on my cheek."

The wind whipped up as he motor-launched over to the island.

As he climbed aboard the old wooden barque lodged on top of the sub, a big wave splashed down the open hatch. Below, in the ancient ships cargo hold they discovered 23 pairs of human skeletons lying in bunks, bones bleached white by eons of salt water. Some skulls had green seaweed Medusa-like hair and ears of barnacles. The bones looked as if their owners had clung together two-by-two like on old Noah's Ark of Christian Biblical lore.

The Captain thought, *our whole earth is a well fitted Ark we dwell on – with a moon large enough to keep us stable, but are its inhabitants unstable?* Could God have made such faulty creatures?

So what really happened? More questions emerged. Why 23 pairs of bones in co-mingled spread? Was this a numerical significance? Did it have any connection to the male 23 chromosomes plus female 23, adding up to the 46 in the DNA of a human embryo? Was this barque's cargo of souls a survival attempt to escape and re-populate the planet after its nuclear annihilation?

Wild speculation flared among the cruiser's crew and scientists.

Postulations poured forth.. Who fired first? Did God get mad because halibut and dolphins screamed for mercy?   Was the sub on a survival plunge to escape? The scientists seemed entranced with the human skeletons on both boats. They were blanched pristine white, lying neatly in their sarcophagus bunks.

Maybe the sub's old log-book would reveal some answers. However, its pages were too faded to talk. But the record did show a bleached out final entry.

It read, "Nations should examine their blemishes in the mirror of Mischief Reef and turn from the reflected image of their own brutality."

Dated April 1, 2248, the log bore the faint remains of a signature in Mandarin.   It looked like, "T. Maru, Captain of the Submarine Kianda #4.

That night, back aboard his science ship, the Captain excused himself from the scientists and their speculations. He retired to the solitude of his cabin and read the final verse of the "Rime of the Ancient Mariner" again ...

"God save the ancient mariner
from friends that plague thee thus --
Why look'st thou so?
-- with my cross-bow
I shot the Albatross."

End

Polarized

The doorbell rang ... and there stood the Chaplain from prison.
This was the third Christmas now he'd come to my door -- come
from prison where Daddy was for killing Mama. Each year he
brought a package from Daddy. Like always, I would not invite
him in. I hated Daddy – never been to see him; never wrote.
The Chaplin extended his hand holding a small package toward me
wrapped in a red Christmas paper.

"Hello Annie," he said, "Your father says to tell you he's very
sorry for what he did and he wants you to have these."

On top of the package, was an old Polaroid Camera photograph
of Mama and Daddy. I looked at the picture -- ripped it in half and
threw it on the wooden porch floor.

Slamming the door – I raced to the bathroom -- slumped down
beside the toilet and cried. I stood up and moved to the sink to
wash my face. A tiny black water spider inside the white ceramic
basin crawled upward on the slick surface.   It slipped backward
and struggled up again. Transfixed, I watched the creature attempt
to escape the abyss. I reached for the faucet handle to flush it down
the drain. Then, I don't know why, I stayed my hand and watched
the spider struggle. It finally climbed out over the rim, down a
crack and disappeared to a fate unknown.

I walked back out on the porch; picked up the torn photograph
pieces and found some scotch tape. I re-positioned Daddy's image
next to Mama and taped my family back together again.

I opened the package the Chaplain brought. It contained a few
sheets of blank white note paper imprinted with the faded image of
a church steeple and cross.

I pondered ... swallowed, then sat down at the table, took pencil
in hand and wrote ...
'Hello Dad'...

End

The Wall

Captain Emerson Drumm of the Military Police, strode into his command post , a scowl on his face,

"Tear down the wall??" he exclaimed like a question, "The Senator in Washington who said that must be delusional." The Captain of MPs at the Iraq Embassy looked around the room. "Did you guys hear that report?"

The other MPs in the Baghdad office had also seen the news on al-Jazzeria TV from Damascus. It gave the latest news from Washington ... but the boss when angry was nobody to cross swords with.   6'4" and steely blue eyes, the captain of their unit often caused those who failed to meet his expectations to back off when subjected to their perceptive intentness.

The second in command of their 230 man police force said, "You're right boss. Baghdad is still damn dangerous. We need the wall ... those Senators back in D.C. shouldn't be criticizing it in public. Don't they know there's still a war here?" He banged the keyboard with rough fingers and flipped the calendar to the new month of June, 2011.

* * *

Two black-robed men stood bent over a wooden table, leaning their hands on its ancient cedar edge. They studied the map laid out before them. It showed the city of Baghdad spread out between the Tigris and Euphrates Rivers.

"The explosives are hidden somewhere on this map," the younger clean shaven man said, referring to large steel drum full of powerful plastic explosives.

The older man removed his visored cap and replaced it with the silk brimless turban of an Imam, a Moslem leader of a Mosque. His face looked like an aging mushroom with a trim white beard.

"The British probably stored the canister in their navy dock here," he pointed to a spot on the bank of the Tigris near the Sarafaya Bridge going over toward Sadr City, an insurgent stronghold.

The younger, smaller man nodded, picked up his back-pack of school books and slung it over his shoulder.

Behind the two men, the plaster wall displayed a framed photograph of an ancient Holy Koran, its well-worn leather cover frayed at the corners, and on the opposite wall hung a modern plastic plaque in English. The Imam had brought the new one back from a trip to Washington D.C. before the war, where he had visited a tourist souvenir store and bought the wall plaque reputed to have hung in an office at the CIA.   It read:
> "When you've gottem' by the balls,
> their hearts and minds will follow."

The Imam, a Moslem cleric, had posted the vulgar plaque on his wall for its shock value to remind all Iraqi patriots that they must retaliate against the hated American invaders here to crush Moslem culture. He wanted to prod patriot minds that although we may have temporarily lost our grip, we will get the infidels back in our clutches. We must not give up.

A cell phone deep in the Imam's overlapping garments sounded a trilling tone. He answered it, "This is Amahd"... He listened, then said to the younger man, "Send out the bulletin".

His son, Daraish, clean shaven, skin the color of light tan patent leather moved to the task of duplicating a hundred bulletins on an old Samsung printer. They would be hand delivered to a select few of their followers. Secrecy was imperative.

The message read:

" July 8, 2011

The success of our mission, to take back control of our streets, is now mostlyaccomplished. The American law enforcement soldier/police have now scaleddrastically back in number to less than 10 supervising officers and all those retreat back

behind their Embassy wall every night. Now we must encourage their further retreat from our sacred land by showing them their Walled Embassy is vulnerable. But do not attack the wall now ... it is too formidable at this time. Await further word.
'Praise Allah.'"

-- Signed, Imam Ahmed Moharrah

* * *

An early sun cast a long pointy shadow on the sandy ground. The dark shadow came from a roof turret topping a tall concrete guard tower which guarded over one corner of the vast new American Embassy. The tower is one of four anchoring the giant putty-colored concrete, blast resistant, steel reinforced wall surrounding the Embassy grounds. Outside the wall, in the ground, a sand fly can't move without being analyzed by electronic sensors.

Into this scene, outside the wall, dwarfed by its 14 foot height, a man strolled along side its base. He wore a loose semi-military jacket open to catch the morning breeze. A visored cap, like that of a ship captain topped his head. His brown bearded face craggy tinted by sun and wind. His name was Ahmed.

"Good morning," Ahmed exclaimed, waving a hand in a friendly gesture up toward the helmeted guard manning his 20 millimeter Gatling gun. The tower guard waved back, then shifted his gaze to a man fishing the Tigris River in an old round shaped rowboat made of palm tree twigs and layered leafs and black waterproof pitch-blend, the same kind of crude boat fishermen had used three thousand years ago in ancient Mesopotamia. Across the river, the far shore blended into a shimmer. A goat bleated as he tore his teeth into an old leather American soldier's combat boot half buried in the hot sand. Little night mice crept back down in their holes to escape the day's imminent heat.

As the bearded one continued his walk, he carefully observed the wall's base which protruded an extra 10 inches out on the sand like a thousand elephant's hooves stomping on holy ground. He studied the wall's concrete massiveness. He had heard tell that the wall's inner structure was laced with electronic sensors ... even his footsteps were now being monitored. How secure, he thought. Just like, the Caliphs of old Arabian Nights had built security around their Harems. He must tell Daraish that the north tower guards add an additional man when changing shift at 6 AM.

The high wall surrounded the new United States Embassy building and its ancillary structures   ... a giant fortified compound the size of Vatican City ...by far the largest embassy in the world, its 104 acres big enough for 84 football fields. Inside the embassy's high walls a small city boomed. In addition to a three story State Department Building, twenty other three and four story buildings, apartment complexes, Army barracks, construction workers' residential quarters, an air-conditioned gymnasium, fitness center with swimming pool, big general PX store with cafeteria and deli, a separate Burger King, a baseball diamond, tennis courts, warehouses full of canned food, our mammoth electricity generators and backups in case of bombing and their own water-treatment plant safe from sabotage.

Tall steel erection cranes flung their long steel arms skyward swinging pre-cast concrete into place the final four story building to house 619 blast-resistant apartments. They housed 500 private contractors like the Blackwater Company and Halliburton construction workers, including dark-skinned workers from Kuwait who blended in with Americans in blue jeans. About 3,500 people lived within the Embassy walls, including a U.S. Army motorized infantry combat battalion of 900 men and their armored Humvees, helicopters and trucks. Captain Emerson Drumm's company of military police also lived there, plus the Blackwater Company's armed guards and private contractors who provided extra security on re-building buildings decimated by war throughout Baghdad's sprawl of 6 million people.

Inside the State Department's main building, Captain Drumm looked out at the construction next door and thought back to when as a kid he had built LEGO blocks into an army tank with green soldiers.

After college ROTC he longed to see the world and bring order to it. His dad's stories of Vietnam lodged in his head like a bullet that could not be removed. So Emerson volunteered for the regular Army as a Lieutenant and now was in his second tour of duty in Iraq.

Jennifer Reed, 31, as slim as her name, longed for knowledge. In college, between volleyball games, she was a serious student, not like some who fell in love with their professors and began to say "shit" instead of darn and heck. She had the slim hips and broad shoulders of a swimmer but walked with a ballerina's grace. She wanted to see the world, so she joined the State Department. She had fallen in love once, but her father didn't approve of her man, insulted him, drove him away and left her with the feeling she wasn't desired because he gave her up without a fight. The memory stuck like a disfiguring scar. When chagrinned, she brushed her auburn hair away from her brown eyes to mask her hurt.

As Assistant to the Deputy Under Secretary for Cultural Exchange, Jennifer Reed's job was to foster American culture and educate those of other cultures. After a crash course in Arabic, she had taken an assignment in Iraq to organize a program of TESOL ... Teachers of English to Speakers of Other Languages.

Now, after four months in Iraq, working in her new post training classes of high school educators so they could establish other schools, Jennifer was bored. She had not stepped outside the wall yet. Her off-duty hours revolved around the swimming pool and gymnasium with their favorable ratio of men to women.

This morning she stood in the breakfast cafeteria line. She glanced up at the menu board, peeking around a tall Army Captain in front of her with an MP arm-band and a 45 on his belt. As they waited, a huge black-bearded Arab in construction blue-jeans struggled to fathom the menu. The Captain looked around.

"You in a hurry?" he said, smiled and motioned his hand forward.

"Thank you, in fact I am late for class." She moved forward.

"What kind of class?"

"English and Arabic." The instinctive movement of her eyes sparked blue.

"I should learn some more of both." His grin crinkled back.

* * *

Jennifer had watched two slide show presentations warning of venturing out beyond the Green Zone, or even farther out in the neighborhoods of the huge city, so she had stayed inside the Embassy wall except for a short sight-seeing tour on an old river excursion boat.

Outside the Green Zone, it's a quick-sand of bugs and old machine-gun shell casings and black robed men with furtive glances, they said. However, she did want to go out and see Arabic culture especially the site of Nebuchadnezzar's Hanging Gardens of Babylon, the birthplace of zero-based numbering system which came to be adopted by the whole world.

Emerson Drumm adjusted his hip-holster, his eye-corners engraved with crows feet peeked over the partition of Jennifer's office cubicle.

"Hi professor, do you want to go see a bazaar in the old Kasbah after work. When do you get off?"

"Great," she shot him her best smile. "It's a good day for old Assyrian culture. Give me ten minutes."

She hurried to log off her computer. Maybe she'd get to practice her Arabic, maybe read some store-front signs. The language of the Quran, the holy book of Islam, was written right to left.

As Emerson maneuvered their armor plated GMC Suburban out the front gate, MP guards recognized their commander and waved him through. A flash of self importance flickered in her head.

"I must tell you", he said, "It's a huge city and the old market is far outside the Green Zone and   could be a little dangerous even after five years since Ambassador Brenner and his team installed the new government."

The Green Zone was the nicer enclave of the old city where many of Saddam Hussein's ruling party of Sunnis had lived and ruled from a palace-mansion cordoned off behind a low wall.   It's also where the Americans had installed the newly elected government under Gov. Maliki ... there in Saddam's old palace.

"How dangerous is it now?" She stared at the recently reopened Baghdad Zoo as they passed, pointing to an elephant and dozens of chattering Meer Cats. They passed an Iraqi police station where local cops saluted as they recognized the embassy MP boss.

"That's the station that just last year was raided by Sunnis who stole their Iraqi police uniforms and identity cards for later use in infiltrating our private zones," Emerson said

"Occasionally it's still dangerous," he added, "as late as 2009 rockets from grenade launchers rained down, even on the Green Zone ... mainly from Sadr City a Sunni stronghold north of the river."

They crossed the Tigris on the Sarafiya Bridge which only recently had been repaired from bomb damage, and entered the old Sunni neighborhood of Bab al-Muadham. Traffic lights were working again. They watched the city crawl by as she practiced reading store-front signs

A hooded figure wearing a burqa with tails flowing behind zoomed by on a motorcycle. Emerson stopped to let a caravan of oil trucks marked Kurdish Oil Co. pass.

"But now," Emerson continued, "seven years after President Bush's "Mission Accomplished" premature announcement -- aboard the battleship, we've turned control over to our trained Iraqi police and troops.

"Haven't we changed the Green Zone's name to 'The International Zone?" she asked.

"Yes, they thought it would purify its image but everyone still calls it 'Green.'"

Now, miles away from the Green Zone, they drove past bomb damaged buildings. Construction cranes of The Halliburton Company swung new machinery into an old electric power plant. Emerson maneuvered slowly thru the narrow crooked streets approaching the old Kasbah market area still in the same location as back in ancient Assyria. They slowed to a crawl, maneuvered through the crowded tenement maze (a travel brochure would call it "Exotic charm") and finally nudged into an empty space near the market.

Near naked kids, already shrunk by Sand Fly Fever pressed in on them with a pitiful plea, "Baksheesh sahib, baksheesh" (money sir, money). Jennifer handed out small 'fil' coin like a nickel. Kids smiled and ran toward a kebob street-vendor.

Beggars, collapsed in helpless heaps on the sand, got no more than a glance from passersby. The stench enveloped your nose

repulsing your senses. The ancient repositories of human waste
and accumulated filth hid behind stucco walls. An air of apprehen-
sion invaded Jennifer's brow.   Kids with hands out trailed Jennifer
like a Pied Piper until merchants shooed them away.

"Beware of pick-pockets, these kids have Velcro fingers,"
Emerson said.

They entered the canvas covered markets like going into a tunnel. They strolled between the brightly colored facades. Booths of
glittering trinkets, Persian rugs, ceramics, leather slippers, sweet
brown dates and raw smelly fish crawled by. Meat offered as edible
by vendors, hung exposed to the stifling heat and swarms of flies
crawling on carcasses. Carts of second hand computers, pirated
DVDs, fruit stands with beautiful green watermelons welcomed
hundreds of shoppers.

As they maneuvered through crowded isles between merchant's
stalls, old bearded men wearing silk Gurkha's turbans and women
with head shawls, droned on in a garbled mixture of Arabic and
Farsi in the stifling hot air. Young clean shaven men sat at a table
smoking Shisha water-pipes. Jennifer hesitated a second at the
heat and smell as brown-skinned humanity pressed down on her.
A walking vendor with a bright red painted clay barrel strapped
on his back offered a paper cup of   freshly brewed herbal tea. She
glanced at Emerson questioningly. He nodded "Yes." She paid for
it and sipped. They wove through the labyrinth slowly. A dirty
bearded Arab looked from deep beneath his hood. He sat behind a
box full of sand offering Sand Readings of your fortune. Emerson
gave him a coin.

"Go ahead, imprint your palm in the sand," he nodded toward
the box.

The man's eyes blazed from deep inside his hood as he
smoothed out the sand and motioned with his hand toward the box
invitingly. He mumbled something.

She strained to understand his words, then said,

"No thanks."

Emerson moved to a booth selling caftans and Jennifer ambled
across the narrow isle to look at multicolored silk scarves. She
fingered one.

"Kam" she said, trying out her Arabic for "How much?"

"I cut the price on that one to 6 dinars, is it not beautiful?" The vendor said in broken English.

A bearded brown skinned man wearing a visored cap emerged from the crowd.

"He's cheating you, offer him 4," the beard said in broken English. She didn't smile but looked away. She had been indoctrinated not to look Arab strangers directly in the eye. It was considered impolite, even arrogant, especially for a woman. The man removed his cap in polite western fashion.

"I had the honor of transporting you and your companions on my little old ship yesterday. I am Captain Ahmed."

"It was an interesting voyage captain, and thank you," Jennifer said as she handed the merchant 4 dinar and swung the scarf around her neck.

The man donned his hat, like a ship captain's cap. His hand then gestured a sort of semi-salute toward the Captain with the MP armband joining them.

"We are launching of our brand new larger ship next week, thanks to help from your Navy," the bearded one said. "My son and I are hosting a celebration party aboard with live Baghdad music. If you could attend we would be honored." He handed them his card.

"Mabrook" (congratulations) Jennifer said.

"That's very good pronunciation," the beard grinned.

In the background the high pitched sing-song of the Muezzin's wailing call to mid-day prayer filtered through the canvas roof.

Ahmad's family had owned two boats, which for many years ferried 80 passengers and freight up and down the Tigris and Euphrates Rivers. Iraqi families had enjoyed taking the excursion boat down to Basra on the Persian Gulf and back on special holiday picnics.

Back in 1942, in WWII, the American army had hired their little ships to carry American airplane engines on their way to their ally Russia.

But in 2003 and 2004 Amahd's precious boats and docks were bombed by American predator drones. Ahmad's family had now waited seven long years for a replacement.

From the upper deck of the pilot house the bearded man pointed to the Tigris riverbank near the Sarafiya Bridge as they chugged past.

"The Americans have rebuilt our old power plant at the base of that bridge," Daraish, his son, said. "They were quick to complete it after they bombed it when the city fell to their army. We think they have a hush-hush navy storage depot there, one they took over from the British."

"Why do you think so?" Ahmad asked, his tobacco darkened teeth displayed themselves.

"Because their patrol boats only go in and out at night," Daraish frowned.

"Let's assume your right ... put the hand-palm-map on it," he said, referring to a sheet of cellophane. Ahmad reached into a table drawer and withdrew the sheet of clear cellophane stolen from the Brits before they left town. Imprinted on the plastic was a man's open palm print in blood red ink, which when laid over the map of Baghdad, the fore-finger pointed to the secret ordinance depot.   Ahmad spread it out flat overlying the map of the city, its imprinted hand-print, in red with fingers spread-out. Sure enough, the fore-finger's tip overlaid the shore abutment of the bridge.

Looking through the imprinted cellophane, both stared at the red finger imprint ... its finger-tip lay directly on a warehouse on the riverside dock.-- the probable point of the treasure they sought, a storage drum full of plastic explosives.

"That must be where the explosives are." A smile of stained brown teeth crackled through his beard like a wolf eyeing a lamb. "We can grab the barrel at night, run it up river and plant it next to the wall."

"It won't demolish the wall, but it should certainly blow a hole in it", Daraish said, shrugging his shoulders as if not sure of the strategic validity of the idea.

Ahmed's eyes burned black. "We'll show them, they think we are puppets but the shadows of our puppets, will envelope them ... praise Allah."

* * *

The following Saturday, Riverboat Captain Ahmads's new riverboat (made in Mobile, Alabama) had cheerful flower vases tied to the hand rails. Smiling passengers and visiting people crowded both decks. Men and women visitors, some barge company employees, back-packing college students from Bagdad University, a Muslim Mullah, engineers from their new Transportation Ministry and their wives and well-wishers all mingled on the upper deck. The Mayor of Baghdad with his bodyguards listened to music drifting up from the lower deck.

"Let's go down," Emerson said.

Jennifer nodded.

They walked down the iron stairs. On the lower deck, a man wearing full length old Arabic costume, served coffee and wine to everyone.

"Your wine tastes delicious," Jennifer said.

"Thank you, it's made from juniper berries, our alchemists were making a wine-like-gin a thousand years before the French." We normally don't drink alcohol but this is a special occasion for our guests.

Emerson raised his glass in a gesture of approval.

A four piece band, including an old Persian stringed instrument, played an old Arabian melody, then switched to a slow shuffling rhythm that could be from an American high school prom.

Baghdad University kids shuffled on the dance floor. A saxophone wailed smooth as campus guys and gals in sweaters and slacks danced defying old ways. Passionate chords entered their veins and the beat came from their pounding hearts. It looked like Saturday night on a campus at home.

An ancient bearded Persian looked on in stoic silence. Emerson glanced at Jennifer and nodded his head toward the dance floor, but she smiled and declined.

Now the music changed again. Another man in a long Arabian robe started singing. The lumbering syllables wailed out over the water. People gathered to watch ... they listened intently.

Imam Ahmad approached, but now he wore his ship captain's handsome tan uniform.

"I'm honored that you could come," his smile inscrutable as a Persian cat.

"Thank you for inviting us." Emerson nodded toward the singer. "What is HE saying?"

Ahmad translated, "Iraq, how sweet he is ... in our hearts is his house ... the future is all for him," then added, "He was very popular on the radio and TV during Saddam Hussein's time in power."

"Let's hope he is popular again," Emerson said.

Now the singer slipped into a new song. Emerson recognized it, 'Al-Salam al-Jamhouri,' their Iraqi national anthem. People joyously joined in, their voices enthusiastic, proud, almost feral, not the voices of subdued vassals.

Off the port side, a 40 foot gunboat, one of the new American-made ones cruised by. An Iraqi navy man in his new black and tan uniform stood beside a deck-mounted tripod topped with the American Navy's newest Gatling gun, one that spit 10 rounds per second. The gunner smiled and waved hello at the revelers.

"That boat is beautiful too, is it not?" Ahmad said nodding toward the gunboat. "It's one of nine now patrolling the rivers, courtesy of your Navy", he smiled an enigmatic Buddha-like grin.

"We want to go downriver with you someday to visit old Babylon", Jennifer said.

"Good", he said, "Even your Bible places early civilization in that area."

She smiled at Ahmad's phrasing, "Your Bible," as if she might not have read it.

Overhead, one of the American Navy's new surveillance Dragonfly Drones hovered like a humming bird.

* * *

As Emerson waited outside Jennifer's classroom, he peaked through the glass door. She looked like a power-point presentation with a pedigree.

As her Wednesday English class at the Embassy ended, one student, approached the teacher and extended his hand ... a handsome slim young man, clean shaven face, his black hair flashed its glow under the neon ceiling tubes.

"Hello Miss Reed, I'm Daraish Ahmad," he said nodding his head politely; "I didn't get to meet you on my father's boat yesterday."

"Hello, your father was so kind to include us ... are you a teacher of English?"

"I hope to be, we hope to open a new high school. We have twenty-two adult students in our English class, both men and women."

What he didn't say was that the location of their two original classrooms out in the Baghdad suburbs, outside the Green Zone was so dangerous because of continued Taliban attacks on those locations that they had to be relocated to inside the Embassy. The schools had become a magnet for al Quieda attacks endangering whole neighborhoods. Al Quieda 'freedom fighters', were fierce guardians of their culture, language and science ... and its corruption by infidels.

As they came out of the class room, Jennifer introduced Emerson to their new young teacher candidate.

"Could you join us for coffee at the cafeteria, Daraish?" Emerson said,

"Thank you", his leather-like face inscrutable. Emerson had seen that same look on street vendors. The black eyes of Daraish darted to Jennifer's face repeatedly like iron balls to a magnet, a clear taint of mystery caught somewhere in the transparency of his forced smile.

* * *

Postwar Baghdad bustled with activity during daylight, but remnants of bombed out houses with shrapnel studded walls, burnt out automobile skeletons and bug infested debris, still showed some old war wounds. However the Arabian charm had begun to resurrect itself. Slender minaret towers and blue and gold domes of mosques rise above the low flat roofs of gray mud-brick houses. Graceful date palms sway over patches of green grass along the banks of the Tigris River. The view was spoiled by the bombed out bridge, its rusting brown steel span still down in the water like the neck of a wounded camel. Tattered awnings stretched from roof to roof across narrow streets, shielding people from the burning summer sun. Waves of shuffling people, and more people riding bicycles, motor-bikes and small automobiles sped past. Large American military trucks and small Fiats assaulted a few tired donkeys crowding the narrow crooked streets.

In contrast, a few new modern steel and glass buildings have replaced a few older bombed out ones. Traffic zoomed both ways on the six lane main road through the center of the city. Modern caravans of trucks now haul oil from the north Kurdish areas, but the rusting remains of Saddam's old 57 millimeter anti-aircraft guns still stood out in the fields, stripped of most parts still pointing their rusting barrels skyward like embalmed giraffes.

* * *

The Imam smiled at the fat oil trucks rolling in from the northern Kirkuk Oil fields. Each truck driver had a second rider, a helmeted "Pesh." The Kurds have their own army, the Peshmerga.

The Pesh carried a Russian AK 47 and looked determined to exact revenge and drive out the infidels. Oil, the new gold, will once again gild over the colorful geometric patterns on the domes of our mosques destroyed by infidel bombs. The Imam's smile turned serious. Allah demands vengeance for the cursed Predator drones that destroyed our homes and spy on us in our back yards. The Imam's anger blew through the hot air like a power boat's back wash through floating jellyfish.

A turbaned man driving a small vegetable-laden truck glared and muttered an Arabic curse between clenched teeth at a helmeted American soldier ... one of the few left. He spit on the hard packed earth scorched by the herringbone of Hummer tire tracks. The street was strewn with shards of plate glass from a car bomb explosion several days ago. However, the JJ Photo Store was open, an Iraqi version of the Wild West photo booth at Disneyland, where American soldiers got pictures of themselves in Arab Robes and headdress.

* * *

Baghdad at night is a different and somber place. The dark narrow streets electric lights still had not had not yet been replaced, decimated by howitzers and cruise missiles. In the south half of Baghdad the Dura Power Plant had been destroyed then only half rebuilt by Americans. In the turbine room, graffiti on the wall read, "Long Live the Resistance". Skeletal hulks of burnt out buildings with faces blown off, still not repaired in the old neighborhoods, loom like ghosts, and construction cranes cranny their necks up like lazy long-necked camels .. all idle for months at a time.

* * *

August 2, 2011 ... al Jazeera Television from Damascus splashed images of blurry faces and summarized ...
"Baghdad car bombs ripped thru Shiite and Kurdish targets in Baghdad and Mosul, killing at least 660 people, wounding more than 200 and feeding doubts that Iraq will emerge as a stable democracy after a decade of war and the new government installed by the Americans. The coordination, sophistication and targets of the attack bore the hallmarks of al-Quieda and its Sunni militants. The blasts were the third this week."

* * *

Ahmad gloated inside his skin. *The invaders would continue to pay... yes they would pay for the deadly drone bombings. The Great Satan would no longer grow fat on our petroleum.* He had worked now for four years trying to unite the Bader Corps of Sunni patriots and the Shiite Dawa freedom fighters, who normally opposed each other on religious doctrine. If they would join forces they could force the Americans to withdraw all their remaining troops.
August 14, 2011 ...Headline.
"Tens of thousands of Sunni Muslims rallied in central Baghdad to protest unfair treatment by the Shiite–led government. They screamed for Prime Minister Maliki to release thousands of Sunni prisoners accused of counter terrorism. American soldiers remained in their quarters in the Embassy."

The Imam was fond of saying, "Our war will be remembered for events and battles that have not yet happened. Their wall will eventually melt like an iceberg on our hot desert sands." "Praise Allah", he declared in his God-to-Moses voice.

The Imam liked to tell the ancient tale of the crusades, when English King Richard the Lion Hearted led his knights into Persia against Prince Saladin. In a meeting to discuss armistice the Persian Prince had said, "Your English swords are not sharp enough to defeat us."

King Richard blustered -- drew out his big iron sword and slashed it down through the wooden table.

Saladin said, "You have shown the strength of your arm, not the sharpness of your blade."

The Arab drew his steel scimitar from its scabbard ... tossed a silk scarf in the air and let it drift down over his blade which easily sliced it in two, as the invader stared in amazement.

* * *

Emerson peeked over Jennifer's cubicle. She wasn't there so he put a red foil-wrapped Hershey kiss on her desk next to the shredder. Every evening at 2100 a CIA guy hauled the shredder out.

Sauntering out of the Embassy building, Emerson looked back at its bunker style facade with recessed slits for windows and filtered air-conditioning against chemical or biological attack. He strolled past the water treatment plant, crossed over to the bomb-resistant recreation and fitness center. Maybe she was in one of the nine Jacuzzis lined up at attention. She wasn't there, but five Jacuzzis were full of soakers incased in cocoon isolation waiting for their next bridge game. He headed for the Halliburton construction worker's apartment building where he was supposed to attend an orientation on understanding Mohamed, delivered by a top sergeant chosen for his voice which was equal parts Darth Vader and earthquake.

It would be his third required lecture for embassy employees. A flop-flop flutter of a twin propeller helicopter sounded outside as the chopper rose from its pad like an albatross with an attitude.

Trucks packed with hundreds of Halliburton construction workers forayed out in the morning to help repair the city's infrastructure. They'd come back within the wall at night like to a medieval walled city.

He returned to Jennifer's cubicle and offered a trip to the Burger King. They ordered a   Vitamin D smoothie and discussed the latest bombing of another building in the Green Zone.

"Their vitriol toward us is understandable," Jennifer's intelligence pushed forward. Her finger pushed her glasses up on her nose ... "It's deep down and festering like heat generated in a compost pile."

"Yes," he said. "They know this Embassy was built for staying ... and they are like cobras raising their heads looking and waiting to strike."

"Well, we're not evil like Rosemary's baby." She stood up and put her hands on her hips to mimic outrage, adding, "You want another yogurt." He marveled at her sense of humor.

A clean shaven guy in the black T-shirt of the Blackwater private Security guards stopped at their table and said "Hi" to Emerson. He introduced Jennifer.

"I thought your Blackwater job here was completed," Emerson asked.

"We no longer guard the Viceroy, but they kept me on here guarding the rebuilding of the Dura Power plant. I'm going home next month. You should join us Emerson. Take early retirement and switch over -- you'll make twice as much money ... plus a big bonus. We call ourselves XE Company now ... and Hart Security is hiring too for a big job down in Darfur, Africa."

"No thanks, but good luck," Emerson said.

He walked away trailing a wake of intrigue from his black T-shirt and slacks that most Blackwater guys wore.

"What did he mean?" Jennifer brushed her hair back

"They had a private contract to personally guard Ambassador Paul Bremer. They called him the Viceroy during the dangerous transition period when he removed the sheiks from power. They didn't like his rulings."

"Yes, then Washington reversed course," she said. "In 2007 they brought in Ambassador Ryan Crocker and General Petraeus who transferred the power back to the new Iraqi government and Sheiks.

"The pentagon used a lot of private contractors and civilian advisors." Emerson's blond eyebrow arched. "Petraeus imported a British woman expert on civilian pacification named Emma Skye and an American civilian named Sadi Orthman, an interpreter. I guarded them here for two weeks, they wanted to go to the Iraqi National Soccer championship game but Petraeus said it was too dangerous, so we all watched it on TV."

"What was it like in the early combat days in 2005 and the Stryker Brigades, and your big Bradley troop carriers out in a battle zone?" she asked.

"We called them Forward Operating Bases or FOB's. I remember in my first tour of duty," he began, "I was assigned to the 1st Armored Division back then. Our Bradley carried eight (two drivers and six guys in back). You'd jump out the back door and, and kick some doors down ... a fearful scream as a woman's kids scrunched down in the corner terrified. The women don't normally look at you directly, but she stared at me with a withering gaze that burned through my Kevlar vest. Her eyes never stopped boring into mine.

At night we motored back to our base behind triple rolls of razor wire and though an occasional mortar bomb landed inside -- it was better than out in the streets ... no worrying about IEDs lurking behind a door to blow your foot off, or booby trapped cars. The base was a busy place ... men and women searching out a sit-down latrine and Coronels busily planning the next plunge out into street combat and timed to return and issue a press release to hovering CNN camera men to make the evening TV news."

Emerson paused, and stared out the window toward the wall. He pushed his cap back on his head revealing a point of blond hair receding.

"My buddy was blown up beyond recognition. At least now, with DNA evidence there will never be another unknown Soldier."

"What an interesting yet gruesome viewpoint." Jennifer shuddered.

"But that was 4 and 5 years ago," he continued, "we have now retrenched behind a gigantic wall."

"Yes", she said, "Ambassador Crocker and General Petraeus reversed course, and placated the sheiks with big money to distribute to their Madi Army and key civilians."

"General Petraeus called it his 'Surge' ... more like a deluge of dollars," he said.

"Dollar diplomacy rides again," she spooned another bite, adding "Isn't fate strange?"

"How so?"

"I mean how the pentagon switched strategy and withdrew out of Iraq almost as fast as George Bush got us in here, back in 2003 ... that was 8 years ago." She licked her spoon.

He pushed his empty ice cream glass away. "We mustn't forget it was retaliation to their 9/11 bombing of New York and the Pentagon, and this new embassy will be here a long, long time"

"You're right," she slurped her last bite, "Our influence in the middle east is still growing."

* * *

Two weeks later Emerson and Jennifer, in exercise jogs, sauntered into the Jacuzzi room. Behind it a small weight lifting room with gymnastic tumbling pads on the floor had become popular. Jennifer followed Emerson in. When he turned and locked the door, she felt her neck vein beat.

His large weathered fingers toyed with the curly tips of her gleaming hair. He is thick and solid. She turned her face into his shoulder and his hand tilted her chin up as he lowered his lips to hers.

She wanted to feel his strength, taste his smell. They collapsed on the mats. She scorched her bare thigh on the rough canvas surface. *Was this real?*

After rolling around, Emerson ended up on top face to face ... her long eyelashes flicked his cheek. Their bodies tangled in a horizontal tango ... slow and smooth, then fast ... hearts finally slowed down..   two souls like tumble weeds on the hot sands of adventure. They wrapped up in two giant white bath towels. His thick chest hair tickled. The hum of eight bubbling Jacuzzis next door gradually faded into the background. She stretched both arms languorously.

"Tell me about your current mission, you were gone three days, I worry about you," she said in low confidence.

"Thank you ma'am." He kissed the top of her forehead.

"The Taliban had stolen a barrel of plastic explosives. They hid it and we've been searching to recover it." he said

"Did you find it?"

"Yes, our army guys captured a sort of coded map ... it's in the form of an imprint of a man's hand."

"A hand?"

"Yes, the whole palm, which when laid over a map of Baghdad, the tip of the fore-finger pointed to where they'd hidden the stuff ... I'll show you."

He opened the folds of her bath towel and pressed his open palm on her pink tummy. He pressed his hand in gently but firmly for two seconds then lifted his hand leaving a white imprint of his palm with five fingers on her transparent skin ... the indent slow to erase itself.

"The map was just like that," he said, pointing down, adding, "May I kiss your hand Madam?" He leaned down ... lips warm.

As his head bobbed back up, she cooed, "You do know how to capture a girl's heart Mon Capitan."

They cuddled under white fluffy towels and listened to the hum of the Jacuzzis. After a mellow snooze Jenifer sat up.

"So, what happened?" She said, kissing his ear.

"The dock night watchman reported some guys were hauling out barrels of explosives. He followed them to the museum of the Hanging Gardens of Babylon and called the army MPs. They called us to join them and we did a joint thrust and re-captured the barrels.

We had a skirmish with your student Daraish and his daddy. They were there trying to haul the barrel out.

Jennifer slipped back into her clothes.

"That's too bad, I liked the boy," she said, adding, "but I thought that museum is off-limits to our Army."

"You're right Jen, that's why Ahmad had chosen to hide it there ... and also why the Army asked us to join them on a combined raid

... the whole thing is hush hush. We captured old man Ahmad but your student Daraish escaped."

She raised an eyebrow. "I thought your embassy MPs aren't supposed to be involved in regular army operations."

"Right again ... but that's why they called us in so that if they were caught, the army could say they didn't officially do it but that we, the State Department, did it. It's that thing called deniable implausibility," Emerson grinned.

"Ain't diplomacy grand?" she said.

"Well," Emerson added, "We're learning how to colonize. The Brits were good at it, the British Empire ruled for a thousand years ... God save the Queen."

"We're doing our part," Jennifer said. "We've rebuilt 2,500 schools and furnished them with 18 million new text books of good ole' American learnin'."

The next few days, they played chess in the library and took more trips out over the old road-bed of the ancient 'Silk Road' where thousands of years ago, caravans carried colorful oriental silk from ancient Cathay west for thousands of miles to Roman Senators for their wives.

But what Emerson didn't tell her was that he had been assigned to follow Daraish and bring him back ... a task that could be very dangerous.

* * *

Shatt al-Arab is a place unlike any other in the world. A hundred miles south of Baghdad the Tigris and Euphrates rivers converge and spread their waters wide over the flat land. Lagoon-like swamps inundate both sides, fed by dozens of shallow wadies sloping down from the low hills into seasonal wetlands.

The widened joint rivers' course for the next 80 miles, known as Shatt al-Arab, flows on south to the port of Basra and the Persian Gulf. Its center stream carries river traffic. But its vast swampy shallows spreads out into a floating city of small house-boats jammed in side by side like sardines in cans. Thousands of families live in shack-like boats floating on the water or just a foot above, on rotting plywood. There are miles of connecting rickety floating walkways and docks crisscrossing the murky lagoons. Little rowboats, fishing skiffs and small power boats churn the wide shallows around these neighborhoods for a radius of 20 miles. More than 90,000 people and families live aboard floating shacks. The CIA thought that's where Daraish had taken refuge, in his grandfather's neighborhood ... a safe haven because he could vanish into the labyrinth of canals and board-walks anytime he chose.

Into this watery maze, Captain Emerson plunged to bring back the Imam's son. Diplomats would call Daraish a provocateur ... but not a dangerous radical. And now with the father in Abu Ghraib prison for a while, and the boy out from under his influence, the CIA suggested he should be given leniency. Moreover, they urged the State Department to treat him as a candidate to be converted or "turned into an asset"... maybe offer a college scholarship.

Emerson changed into old civilian clothes and drove an old small Honda south past ancient towns. A quick scan of a road sign said, "Basra 20 miles". He gripped the steering wheel hard.

Why did I volunteer for this mission? ... bucking for Major? ... or to impress Jenifer?

Basra is reputed by scholars to be the seaport home of ancient Sinbad the Sailor, known to have lived by his wits. But now Emerson stopped by a small town at a dock on the river front.

Daraish's family owned a little gasoline dock and grocery store somewhere here out in the lagoon. Since boyhood he had skipped over the many adjoining docks like his own backyard.

Emerson parked next to a rusting hulk of an abandoned Russian Helix truck, unhooked his belt holster and shoved his 45 inside his shirt.

The river docks teemed with people flitting in and out of weathered store fronts. Emerson paused at a boat repair dock. A dirty turbaned guy with a Taliban dagger tattooed on his forearm flashed a suspicious glance at Emerson's clean shaven face with blond eyebrows. Then Emerson made a mistake, he glanced at his Army wristwatch with its distinctive desert olive tan camouflage wristband, so he pocketed the watch. Never-the-less he offered the guy a dinar for his brimmed fisherman's hat and donned it to cover his blond hair. He bought a tattered fisherman's jacket with exterior pockets which he stuffed with a packet of crackers, candy bars and a small bottle of water.

Sweat soaked his shirt. A fetid smell urged him to get on with the job so he could get out of there. At dockside an old wooden rowboat with a small Honda outboard motor hooked on back undulated on the oil slick water. A sign lying on its wood seat read, "For Sale 65 dinars". Inside the dock shack Emerson haggled and then handed over 60 dinars. The merchant mumbled something to another guy as Emerson bought an extra 5 gallon can of gas and put it in the boat bottom. He bought a flashlight and new batteries. *Jesus! Don't want to be caught in this swamp after dark.* He pointed the boat's bow back upstream into the morass of marshlands

He couldn't trace Daraish's cell phone. No response meant the boy was probably savvy enough to have thrown it in the lagoon. However, the CIA had given him a hand-drawn map. Trouble was, it circled a three mile area around where the family store and gas station might be. He trolled in and out of canals and ancient plywood shacks and wobbly walkways. Women dumped garbage. Gray feathered Teal and small Eagles circled. A mother yelled at kids chasing each other over the boardwalks ... their giggling laughter mingled with a lone loon's oboe solo. The sun burned down like a nuclear reactor in meltdown.

His destination was a red Exxon-Mobil Oil gasoline pump. He didn't know if the store next to the pump had a name on it but the CIA guy said it might be painted a dark blue. Most shacks were just weathered wood, unpainted, but some colorful ones, yellows and greens also dotted the boardwalks which sagged in the middle over rotting pylons just baseball bat thin. Even a motorboat's backwash caused the docks to quiver like on drunken pogo-sticks. Metal pontoons made of old oil drums and hollow bamboo buoyed up some of the shaky structures.

There were no signposts. He cruised up canals, in and out between shacks just a foot off the slimy water. Women threw buckets of goo into the water on one side and scooped up buckets from the other as if it were fresh.

Housewives chattered above the stink. Mosquitoes dive bombed like cruise missiles. Emerson removed his coat.

His makeshift disguise didn't fool the kids. They waved and yelled 'Baksheesh Sahib' ... anyone in a motorboat was a prosperous prospect. They laughed, jostled each other and skipped along the ramshackle boardwalks. The dank smell of rotting fish and human excrement permeated everything.

He cruised in and out and around coves for hours. He stopped at a dock with a Russian Gazprom gas pump and asked if they knew where an Exxon pump was. Two kids jumped in his boat holding out their hands. He showed a picture of an Exxon logo, asked, "Where gas?" and gave them a small coin. They pointed two different ways and as they jumped out, one reached into his vest he had laid on the boat bottom, grabbed his cell phone and ran away over a plywood hurdle. "Damn." His cell phone had become a vital extra appendage, but he oriented himself with the sun slowly sinking in the west and forced back a little twitch of doubt. Maybe Blackwater or private contracting would be better than this.

The sun sank lower. There's a myth that a drowning man sees his life pass before his eyes. Emerson remembered his childhood, holding a fishing rod on his grandpa's little lake. A small fish broke the beautiful lake surface sending ringlets out like radar waves. Sparrows twittered from birch branches overhead.

Now his mind came back to this stinking water as the motor sputtered. A montage of images flashed.

"What would I ask for my last sound of life to be?" Jennifer's voice ... like the soprano in the opera Carmen who lured the soldier and now he must face a firing squad. The shooters hold their rifles steady, steel gray gun barrels extend and seem to grow rounder.

Just then, tadpoles slithering from the slimy bank into the canal jolting him back to the present. A plastic bottle bobbed among the garbage. He tightened his grip on his water bottle. What was he doing here at the bidding of his boss who was bucking for promotion to Colonel and curry favor with the CIA who seemed to call more of the shots now? He had hoped to make Major himself and accumulate enough combat pay bonus to go back to grandpa's farm he would soon inherit. He could run for county sheriff. He reached in his shirt and released the safety on his 45.

Finally, late in the afternoon, his bottle of water ran dry.
He remembered the old rock-lined water well on his grandpa's farm
… how good water tastes from a wooden bucket. Jenifer's image
flickered like an oasis. Late afternoon clouds gathered in a sweltering sky ready to cry. He better give up for the approaching night.
In fact maybe he should consider getting out of here and joining
Blackwater.

Then … there!! A red Exxon gas pump! He dreaded going into
the blue front store behind it. These were tough Sunni neighborhoods. They'd slit the throat of heathen American invaders and
brag about it. He slowed the engine and maneuvered toward
the dock.

A figure bent over pumping gas into a small boat.

He couldn't believe his luck … it was Daraish. Emerson cut the
motor and glided in quietly. The boy glanced at him casually, hesitated, stared … then bolted away jumping across to another dock.

"Don't worry Daraish" Emerson yelled, "I'm not here to arrest
you." His heart pumped. His boat bumped the dock, but he didn't
stand up in the boat as if to jump out and give chase.

Daraish stopped, turned, and unsheathed a leather holster, pulling out a long wicked fish cleaning knife. The color drained from
the boys face as Emerson stared at him.

"What do you want?" He flashed the knife.

"We know you didn't intend to explode those drums. You
were just pressured by others. The school principal asked me to
find you."

"Why's that?' He crouched like Spiderman waiting to spring.

"We've arranged a scholarship to Baghdad University for you,"
he said in a clear voice.

"That's not what I heard." Daraish raised a black eyebrow and
then turned to jump again.

"A rooster might think his crowing makes the sun rise, but he'd
be wrong," Emerson said and grinned a friendly flash. He hoped
quoting the old saying of Sinbad the Sailor might get through to
the boy.

Daraish hesitated.

"The scholarship is real. It's true, let's go back. You can trust
me. You'll be able to serve your people better if you're educated."

The boy paused, his eyes glared ... but after a few seconds he sheathed his knife.

Just then, a man burst forth from the blue door. He wore a turban and looked like Sinbad. He carried an old Scimitar curved sword raised over his head and moved toward Emerson who fumbled inside his shirt for his gun.

"NO!" Daraish raised his hand and yelled some agitated Arabic. He jumped back over to his own dock and down into Emerson's boat

"GO", he yelled.

Emerson twisted the throttle handle; the motor coughed, chugged, caught on and purred its little 10 horsepower out toward the main channel. He nosed the bow south toward where his car was.

"NO", Daraish yelled, "Go north," pointing his hand.

Back at the Exxon dock shrinking in the distance, a boat came out following them. He saw two guys; one was Sinbad, still waving his sword. The sound of the pursuing boats loud motor indicated it would probably over- take his boat.

He nosed north figuring Daraish knew the territory best. They had about a hundred yards head start. Emerson fished in his shirt and drew out his gun.

"Don't kill him, he's my brother," Daraish yelled above the sound of the churning motor, "If you shoot at him I'll jump out of the boat."

"*Damn*" Emerson thought ... *a catch 22 moment*.

"We'll reach our river-patrol base soon, trust me" Daraish yelled. "It's just around the next cove to the right.

A splinter shattered the rear gunwale next to the outboard motor.

"He's shooting at us ... I have to shoot back."

"NO", the boy screamed. They crouched down.

The pursuing boat got closer. Emerson swerved and headed into the cove. There, a hundred yards ahead, a welcome sight. A Navy Patrol Boat appeared -- headed directly toward them. Sinbad's boat veered off – turned and sped away as its trailing wake rocked their boat.

* * *

The next week, Jennifer and Emerson sat in the cafeteria. He gazed out the window as three big black birds circled above the giant embassy wall. A silhouetted guard up in the tower watched as a desert hawk zoomed down toward the blackbirds in a kamikaze plunge.

Emerson shifted his gaze to Jennifer's face. He smiled as if in an enigma.

"Are you worried about the wall," she asked.

"Yes, but not from the Taliban ... it's coming under attack from a different and more potentially damaging source now."

"How so?" She removed her glasses.

"Two congressmen and a Senator back in Washington are saying, 'Tear down that wall!' like President Reagan said years ago about the Berlin wall."

"Do they think it's bad public relations?"

"Yes, especially since in the last year the north face has become a billboard for Yankee-Go-Home graffiti."

Jennifer munched a spoonful of chocolate frozen yogurt. She thought back to the graffiti of East Los Angeles which, though critical, became artsy and creative, but these wall-words are not art ... they're loathing hate.

"So now," Emerson said, "Now only a few years after kicking their doors down, kidnapping their husbands and terrorizing their kids, we have retrenched ourselves behind one big wall, and the daily target is to convert enemies into friends."

"Don't be so cynical. We are still dominant in the world." She kneed his knee under the table, adding, "And who better than us should be the world's teacher."

"Yes, but let 9/11 of each year be our Red-Alert Day." She said referring to the attacks on New York. He kneed her back.

* * *

But not all was somber. Now after long months of teaching Iraqi kids English and looking into their beautiful young eyes so eager to learn, things looked rosy ... literally rosy.

It was the talk of the Embassy. After only nine months of absorbing Babylonian culture together Jennifer and Emerson announced they were getting married.

Red roses from the Embassy floral shop and white daisies from the Euphrates Riverbank flanked the center aisle ... the first marriage in the new Embassy ... and consecrated under a mural of a Drone missile. Jennifer and Emerson were celebrities. First, Emerson got credit for unmasking the bad guys and protecting the Wall... and now the first wedding in an overseas embassy in many years. Daraish came from Baghdad University and gave them a Shi Sha water pipe with two smoking stems.

The Assistant Secretary for Cultural Affairs diverted her flight from Tel Aviv to Baghdad to anoint her blessings at the wedding.

The newlyweds drove out from the wall to the al-Rasheed Hotel in the Green Zone in a Humvee with the words **"Just Married"** scrawled on the hood in white whipped cream. Ninety-two U.S. Embassies around the world blogged and tweeted.

* * *

Now in 2011 the American image around Baghdad is not so much American helmeted soldiers who looked like a Martians to their kids, but rather the burly bearded faces and tattooed arms of private contractors from Texas and Tennessee working to rebuild the city's infrastructure. Throughout Iraq old tribal/religious factions are again swarming like mad Meer Cats to see who gets the spoils and dollars of war and its spawn. They wait; confident the wall is built on quicksand of their creation.

Back in Washington, State Department and Pentagon planners coin new terms like "Targeted Surgical Strike" by drones and 'Hegemony' for empire building.

* * *

The week after the wedding, the newlyweds moved into a new apartment inside the wall. Captain Drumm rushed to the Balard Air Base where a thermite car bomb had been detonated killing two workers unloading a C130 cargo plane.

"Round up the usual suspects," he ordered.

MPs promptly sped to the Imam's home. Inside, they gazed at two wall hangings. One, an ancient charcoal drawing of Saladin wielding a curved sword made of Bagdad steel ... and inside the Imam's office, a framed plaque in a little niche above the computer. It was Rudyard Kipling's poem, 'The Young British Soldier"

"If ever your wounded and
fall on Afghanistan's plains,
The women come out
to cut off your remains.
Jest roll to your rifle and
blow out your brains,
and go to your god like a man.

* * *

Yesterday a robed bearded man detonated himself at the Embassy wall's main gate.

The Muezzin's evening call to prayer echoed above the wall. Americans scurried back into their fortified cocoon, collected over- seas bonuses and waited for their next pay grade level.

End

Unison and Unity

Antony carried himself proudly, head up seeking success like the loyal soldier he was. Now he had a mission. His knight's armor fully intact, armed with an acute sense of smell and nobility

It would be a long charge into adversity -- through muddy earth. His six legs churned like pistons through the mire in an unthinking thrust. Her pheromones had radared her location. She wanted him ... gave him a sweet aroma. Suddenly she was just ahead in the dim dark. The outline of her two-segmented body, haloed by four diaphanous wings glowed gossamer. He knew his mission – Kamikaze yes, but glorious for their culture's survival.

He would overcome. He would endow her with a future family -- a forever civilization. Now she spread her four membranous wings for lift off into her marriage flight. He sprang -- clamped his muscled legs around her sticky body and they spiraled to the earth. Driven by nature's earthly essence, he used the large caliper claspers at the rear of his body to hold their genitals together. In a swift precise movement like a guided missile he completed his God- given task.

Antony knew he had a one way ticket -- knew he would die soon, but he was satisfied. He had played a crucial role in producing a potential progeny that would propel life for years. She, now fully fertilized, would produce thousands of offspring in her seven year reign there in her royal chamber. Her children would show immense capability -- worker ants, soldier ants, carpenter ants, harvesters and milk cows. They would protect her from the stings of marauding fire ants.

Antony felt like a Marine ... The Proud. The Few. Mission accomplished! They called him Father Antony. His future family will build tall anthill skyscrapers, the equivalent of erecting a hundred Empire State Buildings. Underground, their labyrinths of earthly chambers, tunnels, dens and lairs would dwarf King Solomon's Mines - achievements by human scale of excavating a dozen English/French Chunnels.

Ten thousand workers overcame adversity... functioning in unison and unity. There's a difference between unison and unity. You can tie two cats together and throw them over a clothes line. You'd have unity but you certainly would not have unison.

Ants coordinate in both unity and unison as a finely organized team to perpetuate their civilization.

Now, as his cartilage disintegrated, Antony smiled.

End

What's In A Name?

Millbur's slim but sinewy body quivered. He felt like a pigeon
trapped inside the ancient brick chimney of the old horse stables.
Fat drops of sleet, rare for southern California, plopped into
a zinc bucket set below the eaves to catch rain water. Milbur
Vandos, the stable boy, winced. He hated both those names he
was saddled with. He wished for a different life. He wanted to
rise like the sun breaking thru the morning fog.A colt nickered
and tossed its brown head breaking the dream. Horses make a
variety of sounds -- a raspy cough, a full throated whiney snort
when infuriated, or a guttural-like resonance when pleased. After
brushing the horse's long sleek flanks, Milbur jammed the brush
and currycomb together and reached his bony fingers up to put a
halter over its head and lead the 2 year old Thoroughbred out for
his morning walk.

A little too tall for a jockey at 5 ft. 7 in. and now also above
a jockey's weight, he wore a jockey's cap with spiky brown hair
protruding. Milbur just galloped horses around the exercise ring.
He hated the term 'Exercise Boy.' He led the colt back into the stall
where he enjoyed the aroma. He cleaned up some grooming tools
and saddles. The saddle soap and leather cleaner, normally a pleas-
ant smell, suddenly became horse shit and the straw on the floor
seemed dirtier.

It had been four years since he got back from Vietnam and he
still worked at Santa Anita race track as a stable boy and played
poker with the jockeys like a hooked addict.

"Make me an assistant trainer," he had asked the boss.

"I'll think about it," was the perennial answer.

Why couldn't he climb the ladder of life? Was it fear of failure
like a gangrene that slips into your mind like a spy?

Milbur resembled Desi Arnaz, the TV star with his light olive skin from his Mexican mom and his father's walnut hair which rippled over his ears like burnt corn husks.

He longed for someone around the track to address him as Mister Vandos rather than Milly or "boy," which always made him feel as insignificant as a horse fly flitting around unwanted. A slight limp from a horse kick, and his oversized baggy pants and shuffling gait projected a touch of pathos almost like a Charlie Chaplin character of old silent films.

After the Army he had studied literature and public speaking at junior college, but he still lived at home with his mom in an east L.A. ghetto.

He read employment ads every day ... and knew the sting of rejection. Other Hispanic guys around the track blamed the "Tortilla ceiling", but Milbur, though quiet in manner, had plans to break that barrier.

And now it was confirmed by his horoscope. This morning his Aquarius reading said, "You have the ability to move an important relationship or situation forward. Do not hesitate ... over-thinking could become a problem.

The phone rang. Milbur answered.

"Who is this?" ... the gruff voice said. He recognized it as the owner of a horse named "Moneymaker" brought in yesterday.

"This is Milbur, Mr. Gatsch, may I help you?'

"I left a brown envelope on the chair next to my horse stall ... bring it up to me ..in the clubroom please."

"Yes sir." He'd never seen the inside of the owners' clubroom. Even top jockeys weren't normally invited into that inner sanctum of owners' exclusive domain. Norman Gatsch, a rotund man with owl eyes behind tortoise shell glasses grabbed the envelope from Milbur's outstretched hand with a terse. "Thank you, what's your name boy?" he said, hardly glancing up

"Milbur, sir." He took the dollar bill from the outstretched hand. A couple of people stared at him. Milbur wondered what they saw ... a narrow framed man in muddy blue jeans frayed at the heels and an old jockey cap on his head, hair down to his neck. They looked at his clothes, not him ... at his shoes. They did not like his intruding on their turf in the sky. They laughed and their laughter washed about him. The laughter came from a crude joke Gatsch told while pointing out the wide glass windows, through which the crown princes and their women watched the races from on high.

Milbur remembered the contemptuous looks others had given him long ago back in Barstow California out in the desert as a kid. "Get 'outta the way Boy," they said. And even in the army they made him a cook, a dirty job in a smelly kitchen where guys bitched about the food he worked hard to prepare.

But now this new contact with the big man and a favor done for him ... now this would be his ticket upward. Smoke from expensive Havana cigars drifted into Milbur's face. He liked the heady aroma.

As he left the club, he glanced out the giant window to far below to view the double ovals of two race tracks, one within the other, one grass and one clay, resting there, waiting for the thoroughbreds and the rich people who owned them.

But Milbur wasn't jealous. He remembered his dad had said, "A jealous man poisons his own dinner and then eats it."

Norman Gatsch, a big movie mogul, had named his new two year old colt "Moneymaker" because he bought him the day after his latest film cleared $26 million ..not a blockbuster but enough to maintain his status among the top film producing studios. Milbur desperately vowed to "Be somebody" in life. He put in extra work hours, scrounged carrots and apples from the horse treat box to save money, drove his ancient Ford to the library almost every other day to read. He purposely avoided poker games and shooting craps with the jockeys. His mom said, "They're a bad influence, like a chloroform cloth laid on your face."

Milbur's mind flashed back as a cook in the army when they cast out spoiled milk and garbage in the trash. Well he wasn't garbage ... he'd show them!

Two weeks later, after walking a long-legged colt and bringing him back in, Milbur ran to the men's room. As he came out, the owner, Mr. Gatsch, who had entered   a 2 year old in a race tomorrow, stood by his horse's stall with an injection needle in his hand. He dropped it in a bucket. As he came out of the barn Milbur picked up the syringe, smelled the tip and followed Gatsch outside.

"I think you dropped this, Mr. Gatsch, and might not want it lying around for others to get hold of."

Their eyes met. Both knew the importance of the act. A silent bond was sealed.

"Thank you" Gatsch said as he extended his hand and took the damaging evidence.

"There are other ways to help this horse win. I know how to make him give his best," Milbur said.

Gatsch raised a bushy eyebrow and lit a cigar

"What do you suggest?" He blew smoke in the boy's face.

"I could be your trainer ... I'd even live in the old barn out at your house. I know horses. With proper care this horse could have a chance to win the Santa Anita Derby next year. You pay me what you think is fair, any thing more than I make here is welcome."

The next day, Milbur dragged his duffle bag into Gatsch's barn. He hung some old fashioned fly paper strips from the rafters and collapsed on a foam mattress in the corner.

Milbur pondered, *This is a transition moment, I'll take a new name,* he thought as if an epiphany. It's an opportunity, a rare chance to boost his climb up the social ladder, like being dealt a full house, a new name, one that brings respect .. a transformation both internally and externally ... like Saul changed to Paul, or Sam Clemmons to Mark Twain. He pondered the new name of 'Carnegie,' after the famous steel tycoon. After all, many in Hollywood changed names. He researched the library for Andrew Carnegie's background back in Pittsburgh and found a cousin named Steven. Yes, Steven Carnegie would be his new name.

He bought new gabardine slacks, got a short haircut and discovered that Gatsch himself had dropped the "Stein" from his name years ago. People in motion pictures, or as they say, cinematography, often wear a double face mask as their life blends joy and pathos of screen life with real day to day living. Hollywood behind the sound stage struggled with the blood of stars and directors and business deals and smashed egos.

* * *

From the front, Gatsch's big house looked like Tara, Scarlet O'Hara's colonial mansion in *Gone with the Wind*. Six white Corinthian columns overhung a broad setback veranda. In the side yard, plump oranges dot a small grove of trees like a checkerboard. By a pond, a weeping willow's filmy branches hung like tattered sails on Yankee Clipper ships.

Half a foot-ball field farther out back, an old weathered two-story horse barn sat behind a tattered wood fence like a back movie lot. An ancient wooden windmill tower still pumped water up into a round galvanized metal tank. Two colts, heads bent down drank in the foreground. A five-acre field of green grass trailed off into the San Fernando Valley. In fact, Gatsch had filmed several movie scenes here.

A week later, activity hummed in Gatsch's backyard some three hundred feet away by the tall green poplars. Steve wondered if Gatsch would accept his change of name.

He decided to test his new identity and acceptance. He donned a sport coat and stepped out of the barn.

As he approached the expansive concrete apron around the Olympic size swimming pool, tanned bodies thrashed around like a covey of thrushes ... three young teenagers flopped in the pool. Rita Hayworth, whose real name is Concino yelled at her kid to stop splashing water out on people. She turned to resume talking to Katherine Grayson (real name Zelma Hedrick). Up on the high diving board, former Olympian Buster Crabbe, flexed his biceps now 18 years after his role as Tarzan and Flash Gordon.From the water below, Crabbe's college-boy son bellowed a Tarzan yell, good-naturedly to mock his dad.

Gatsch waddled toward him, toes outward like clowns feet. Steve waited for a negative reaction to him being here, not the barn. Gatsch glanced at him and continued expounding to every-one about making a picture of the planned trip to the moon that President Kennedy had just announced.

"253,000 miles," he waved his hand up toward the sky, "What a production!"

"Put a woman astronaut in it," his wife said, waving at their daughter in a new bikini, slightly veiled under a gossamer robe.

Gatsch glanced at him again. Milbur couldn't read the boss's reaction but didn't interpret it a scowl so he relaxed and decided to go further.

From the pool Milbur, now in his Steve mode, sauntered into the house. He fished an olive out of the hors d'oeuvre tray and popped it in his mouth.   Centered above the entrance to the living room, two sculptured plaster-cast faces, watched over the scene, one smiling and one frowning -- the masks of the muses looking down to view mortals' changing moods, happy or sad. He stared at the faces. They merged together into each other. Today, Steve chose to think the smiling face beckoned.

He focused on Jane Marshall, a fading musical star. She lifted a mint julep from the butler's tray and strolled out the front door to the shaded porch. She fluffed her auburn hair, shoulder length. Her lemon cashmere sweater clung in all the right places. Men's and women's eyes followed her. There was something animal in her slender slink -- what Gatsch called Star Quality.

Steve maneuvered casually out behind her. He smelled smoke as she lit a king size cigarette and blew a cloud from pursed lips and waved the weed upward, Betty Davis style. She sat in a wicker rocker, one of four. Two were occupied by women discussing Marylyn Monroe's death. The chair next to Jane was vacant. What luck .. he sat down .. and glanced over. Her face was wrinkle free but for little crows feet etched in her eye corners. A small collie nudged her lemon slacks at the knee. She stroked its head. A cool breeze licked Steve's skin as if to say, "Go."

"Hello," he said quietly, "I loved you in *Three Coins in a Fountain*. Was filming in Italy fun?"

"Yes, but hot ... God, that was years ago." She flashed a professional half-smile. She glanced down at the diamond crusted watch on her wrist.

"Clocks are shackles on our dreams," he said

"What are you, one of Gatsch's script writers?"

"Steve Carnegie," he said, holding out his hand. "Naw, I'm just his horse trainer, but I'd like to write. "

"My driver is late," she said

"I clock horses - clocks are for horses not humans. I don't even wear a watch," not revealing he just pawned his to buy his new Brooks Brothers sport coat.

"Tell that to Gatsch. He's got us working overtime." Her eyes twinkled through lavender eyeliner. She had to be pushing forty-five and just divorced from a celebrity husband in a messy paparazzi scene ending up on front pages.

She flicked her cigarette again, like she couldn't act without one in her hand.

A white Lincoln Town car wheeled into the circle drive, squeezed between two Cadillacs and edged a whitewall tire up on the manicured green lawn.

An arrow-faced tan fox with raccoon eyes with gray hair exuding from under his peaked chauffeur's cap walked unevenly to the porch and stumbled up the steps. Jane stood up. Her cashmere body shimmered, highlighting a figure, now a bit more than the standard uniformity of Paramount's guide for chorus girls ... 32 1/2 bust, 23 waist, 34 hips; 12 1/2 calf. Even Venus DeMilo's 29" waist couldn't get a job at Paramount in the old days. She had ridden the bus to the studio chorus stage for two years at $170 per week before being chosen for bigger roles and stardom.

"I'm not going with you George, you've been drinking," she said ... Go sleep it off, but first call me a cab"

"OK, you're a cab," he slurred a half-giggle.

"I'm going to tell Amanda on you, go on home," she said, like lecturing a child. As he headed off, she continued, "I'd fire him, but I can't do without his wife ... she's my right hand since back in the early days,"

Here was opportunity.

"My little old Ford's around the side, can I offer you a ride back to Beverly Hills?"

She turned to look at him. Her eyes were blue, not just blue but delft, aquamarine and cobalt all at once.

When she answered, "Yes, thank you," his temple throbbed.

On that ride to her home, her natural conversation and charm fascinated him. She was genuine. That's what the camera saw. Gatsch had a skill in recognizing star quality.

Two weeks later at another lawn party Milbur, now continuing his new role as Steve, talked to Jane about being highly connected to wealthy horse owners back on Long Island where the Belmont Stakes are run, and his great grandfather, Andrew Carnegie, had a summer house near the Teddy Roosevelt home. Steve bragged about attending a party in the Roosevelt home. Unfortunately, Gatsch overheard him.

"Don't let him in the next lawn party." He overheard Gatsch say to Jonesy, his black chauffer and guard.

Jonesy came to the barn and delivered the message.

"Why you want to impress her anyway," he added. "She's poor white trash gone uppity. Her first film was '*Jungle Goddess.*' It flopped and almost made a fool out of her. Wardrobe pushed up her boobs and the director ordered her to make guttural grunts between her lines, she couldn't get a serious role for 18 months."

Finally Gatsch sold her contract to Warner Bros. where she had a big musical hit. But stardom is like a revolving Ferris Wheel, you don't stay on top for long. Warner Brothers was working on a musical named Brigadoon. She auditioned and was turned down, then Gatsch hired her back for a couple of minor roles.

* * *

Steve wanted to show off his new seersucker sport coat. He drifted along Wilshire Boulevard, past a health food store serving vegetarian cuisine, past the Karma Bookstore and a window offering batik and Mexican Wedding shirts speckled like pimento. Today he could celebrate.

He entered the Beverly Wilshire Hotel and headed toward the bar. Through the glass door he saw Gatsch in the barroom. He was joined by Louis Mayer, head of Metro-Goldwin-Mayer. Now Jack Warner of Warner Brothers joined them. *Are they plotting a merger?*

Curiosity gnawed at Steve as he maneuvered to a chair behind a giant green plant near them.

Voices leaked through the Palm leaves.

"Darryl said he'd be here," Warner said. Just then Darryl Zanuck, head of 20h Century Fox, came in.

They chatted, then asked Zanuck to volunteer as their industry spokesman before the newly scheduled congressional hearing in Washington. They wanted Zanuck to be their representative because he is a Christian rather than Jewish like most studio heads. Some had memories of parents or grandparents back in Germany. They're aware of the prejudice that will be reflected on them if they appear before the cameras of a Washington Congressional investigation.   Some studio heads are still very sensitive to the charges, just as ten years ago when concern arose over a few writers and directors who might have had Communist leanings. Now Robert Taylor walked in and joined the movie moguls.

Steve recalled that Taylor had gone back to Washington to testify back then, as had Ronald Reagan, then a Democrat, and President of the Screen Actors Guild.

Hollywood corporate heads had cause to be concerned back in the late 1950's ... not just competition from growing television, but worry about Congress snooping into the backgrounds of writers and directors. Many had been subpoenaed to testify, hauling them before a House Un-American Activities Committee to scrutinize their lives for supposed communist leanings. Many back then had faced the farce and damage of Senator Joseph McCarthy's unfounded charges. They still chaffed at those slanderous accusations. It was remembered as the 'Inquisition in Hollywood.'

But that was ten years ago ... back when Ring Lardner, the writer, had testified honestly before the committee and was banned from being employed. He had to move to Mexico and write under an assumed name. Others wrote under different names, including Dalton Trumbo who used the name of Robert Fitch until the ban was finally lifted in 1959.

Some had moved to Mexico just to avoid being subpoenaed, because just to appear in Washington before the TV cameras, guilty or not, was damming to their careers.

Now in the bar, Zanuck said he'll think about going to Washington again if the rumored hearings come again. He has friends there from when he made training films for the Army years ago in WWII.

As Steve walked away from the hotel, his mind shifted to his own current problem and a new unexpected twist of fate. A week ago Gatsch's horse "Moneymaker" had died. The vet said it was from a natural sickness, but Gatsch, looking for a scapegoat blamed Steve for not detecting the problem sooner. Then the gardener told Steve he overheard Gatsch tell a guest he was going to expose Steve's masquerade to Jane.

A week later at Jane's Beverly Hills home she was morose.

"Gatsch negotiated my contract downward," she said in a low petulant tone.

"He doesn't recognize star quality." Steve said.

Her voice rose, "He insulted me further by putting in a clause which demotes my billing credits."

Steve knew she meant her name would no longer be shown above the movie title, but below it in billing and advertising, a demotion that would be grist for the Hollywood gossip columns as well as less money.

"You'll always have top billing with me," he said, knowing her ego needed repair.

"Thank you Steve ... just help me buy a race horse, we'll beat him at the track."

Steve's eyes glowed at the thought and welcomed his new status. *Now he had her confidence.*

"We'll beat him," he echoed.

The next day at Jane's Beverly Hills home they sat in front of a glass coffee table with a *House Beautiful* on top. She wore a sweater and slacks the shade of polished pewter conforming in all the right places. Her cigarette glowed once more as she waved it in the air.

"I'll show him ... my pictures made the most money he ever had. We'll beat him at the track," she repeated from yesterday.

"I know just the horse," he said ... seeing a fish-in-the-barrel opportunity to make big money by recommending a nag whose owner would pay him a big fee to tout his old has-been sire.

"Do you have a horse in mind?" she blurted.

Quick as a lizard's tongue he said, "I do."

On the inner track circle, the grass one, at Santa Anita, they watched her new horse, "Go Go Man," run his practice sprint.

"Isn't he beautiful," Steve said as the horse rounded the half-mile pole. Then, "Oh No." the horse stumbled, fell and couldn't get back up ... its leg broken.

She cried when they put "Go Go Man" down.

What luck, Steve thought. *Jane will receive the proceeds from the Insurance on the horse, and I am saved from being exposed as a crooked tout.* A Jiminy Cricket on his shoulder whispered, "You lucky bastard, you don't deserve her."

Steve vowed to help get her a good horse, if she would trust him again.

* * *

A week later Steve came to Jane's house to discuss buying a new Thoroughbred colt. Her big old Spanish style house was modest for Beverly Hills. The walls displayed artwork of children playing on the beach, ballet dancers and family photos, but were remarkably free of Hollywood stuff ... no large photos of her, like adorned many stars walls. His mother had worked in some stars homes. Steve remembered her words ... "You can tell a lot about people by what's hanging on their walls."

Jane rose and undulated toward the kitchen. There is still a certain languor of her legs in tight slacks. *Maybe I shouldn't have cheated her, she might find out I made a huge pay-off on the sale,* he thought.

Steve restrained himself from reaching out to touch her.

She smiled at him as if she knew his urge.

"Maybe Gatsch will make another musical," he said hoping to cheer her up.

He showed her a photo of an excellent 2 year old colt.

"Isn't he a beauty?" he said. But she glanced away.

"I know Gatsch isn't going to make a musical again, only MGM can afford to make them now," she waved her cigarette, "but I could succeed in other jobs especially in the promotion department, but he won't let me."

"I didn't know you could do that."

"I studied English at night school when I was in the chorus and worked part time in the studio advertising department.

I story-boarded some layouts for some scenes that would reduce production expenses ... but he hardly looked at them."

"Have you submitted any ideas recently to the guys over in the Advertising Department?"

She pulled a paper from the drawer and waved it.

"Yes, I wrote this to Gatsch as a sample," she read aloud. "In film promotion we're forced to write glowing adjectives to convey mock authenticity -- exaggerated ads that lure the public to the box office. We're required to write low brow teasing titillations on movie posters that woo our basic need for love and thrills and seduce us like salivating Pavlovian hound-dogs to see the latest movie."

She looked up at Steve, arching an eyebrow, waiting for approbation.

"That's really good," he said. But thought, *it's actually bad, because movie promotion has to be titillating. Luring people to buy tickets is life's blood. Half of all movie productions are financial failures.*

"Just once I'd like to have a chance to write a scene," she blurted. "I'd replace the imbecility of, 'Love means never having to say you're sorry,' with 'Love means never having to say your ugly,' but nooooo, they still expect me to be a sexy queen bee exuding her special odor to lure people to opening night by appealing to prurient interests."

"You are right," he placated. "I bet you could write a winning plot." He sat down across from her ... "one with characters like you and me for example," he paused, smiled an impish grin and continued. "Why did we meet? What lucky chance ordained it? It may be that we're like two rivers that converge into one, our own unknown inclinations impelling us forward in the surge." He narrowed his eyes, chidingly. Thank God she cracked a smile.

"You are a fantasy writer," she grinned and lit a cigarette.

She rose and edged over to the window. Across the street a van with a driver, just a shoulder in the window and a head with a visored cap, a paparazzi looking for a shot of anything he could peddle to the tabloids. She blew smoke toward the window.

"Do you want me to go out the back way so they won't see me?" Steve asked.

"Yes, please do, but first tell me how to select a Thoroughbred, I still want to beat Gatsch at the track. Should I buy a colt or a proven racer?"

"Come to our barn and I'll show you the fine points of a race horse. Gatsch has two of them. You can come by the back road which doesn't go by the big house ... how about tomorrow afternoon?"

She flicked ashes into a crystal glass ashtray ... adding "You're on."

An orange-yellow sun hung low just below the tree tops and shafts of light broke through the foliage and set the lazy creek on fire. Steve ran out to meet her convertible as it rolled to a stop in front of the old two story dairy barn.

As she stepped out, sequins sparkled on her loose fit jeans.

"Welcome to my castle fairy princess."

"Just call me Goddess," she grinned.

In the barn, they approached the big Thoroughbred stallion's stalls. 'Giant Step' stood quivering, stiff ears forward, eyes wide open so their whites flared against his chestnut red nose.

"He likes you, you can tell by the way his ears point forward," Steve said, adding, "They go backwards when he's angry or fearful."

An excited inner speculation flushed his brain. She was here beside him.

"I like him," she said after stroking the sleek muscles down toward his flanks.""He's genuine, not like Gatsch."

Steve decided to gamble.

"I do know horses, but I want to get straight with you. My name isn't really Carnegie, its Milbur Vandos."

"Well, what's in a name? Mine's Rosie," she smiled, adding, "and besides, a stage name isn't a sham of moral pretension, it's just good business."

"I'm so very glad to meet you Rosie," he grinned extending his hand. They shook in an exaggerated single stroke up and down motion. Then freed-up and grinned."You've got a good grip for a girl," he said, knowing she had played a bit part in 'Meet Me in St. Louis' where that phrase was said to Judy Garland by the boy next door.

"Where do you live Steve?" she asked bringing him back to the present.

"Right here," he blurted, "And in my kitchen I'm preparing a sumptuous dinner." He pointed to an old electric hot plate. He skipped over and grabbed two apples from a box reserved for horse treats.

"Fried apples," he announced as he sliced them into a skillet and added a hunk of   butter which sizzled a song.

"Fried apples," she mused; "I haven't had them in years, my mom also made them back in Georgia."

The skillet crackled and a tart apple cider aroma tickled noses.

"Georgia? ... Sho nuff honeychile," he said.

"Why yaay-uuss," she mimicked.

"Well, I don't have any wine to offer, but I do have Georgia's true native drink   -- Apple Jack from Georgia apples." They nibbled the warm sweet apples and saltine crackers. They sipped Apple Jack.

"'OOhh, how good but potent," she said as she swallowed the burn.

"It's for 'sippin,' not for 'swiggin,'" he said, adding, "Out here in California they call it by its fancy French name, Calvados."

Quiet settled down augmented by a barn swallow's chirping.

"Do you have a family Steve?" She brushed a golden strand away from her forehead.

"Sure do" he exclaimed ..."You want to see them?" He pointed up at the half open loft ceiling, up where hay bales were stored.

In a sudden reckless moment Steve jumped up, vaulted over the chair and skipped over to a ladder slanted up against a rafter in the opening of the ceiling. He climbed half way up to the loft, stopped and looked back down at her.

"Come on," he beckoned, "Jungle Goddess 'fraid of high trees?" he mocked."There's a great view from the top."

She stood up. "I love tree houses."

As her sequined jeans kneed up over the ladder's top rung, a double-tailed barn swallow fluttered past her face and out the opening where hay bales were loaded in.

"Come see," he said pointing up to a hay bale up on the next higher level. She giggled as they climbed up on top of bales stacked three levels up higher like stair steps.   He picked up a handful of straw and brushed away a spider web in the wooden angle-joint of the rafter.

"Look," he pointed a finger.

There, nine inches away, an oval bird's nest - three speckled eggs like sky blue marbles lay in the nest- one cracked slightly as if to soon hatch. She gasped at their fragile beauty.

"They're the color of your eyes," he whispered.

She stared at the eggs in silence, then the mother swallow flew back in – and screamed, "Leave my babies alone!"

They scrambled down a level and sat on a hay bale. He jumped down to a bale a level below her, and sat cross legged looking up at her like an admiring fan. Pigeons cooed from up in the rafters. He pointed up.

"That's Bing and Diva my duo of pigeons," he said, then his grin turned somber as he saw her eyes tearing-up.

"What's wrong?" He reached a hand up as if to console, but hesitated, didn't dare touch. Instead, he gulped as she reached out, took his hand and slid off the upper bale to   plop down next to him.

She sobbed softly, "I'm losing my baby ... my daughter wants to go live with her father."

"I'm so sorry," he whispered.

His fingers reached out and touched her shoulder then lingered, toying with the curly tips of her auburn hair. She turned her face into his shoulder. His arm gently circled her slim waist. Silence surrounded them for a moment. They leaned back against the bales. He let the thrill of her pour over him. At some indefinable call of instinct, he couldn't stop. He touched her cheek then stroked her jaw lightly sliding his hand along her jaw line. She looked up and he kissed her lightly on the lips. Their eyes interlocked, then feeling a response, he kissed her again, deeply. His hand moved to cup her breast.

"This is a little scary," she whispered, letting her head fall back. She touched his face with her finger tips. He lowered his lips to hers. Their arms circled each other. Their eyes half open, watched each other then she closed hers as their mouths met and mingled. The straw was so itchy ... they scooted over onto an old horse blanket. The world shut out. Excitement opened their bodies ... the horses whinnied . After a time, they lay quietly ... listening to the birds warble. She asked, "How old are you?" in a low tone,

"Forty-two ... why? Didn't you like my performance?"

"You won an Oscar," her grin united them again. They melted together and drifted into sleep.

A dim shaft of light from an electric bulb below cast a glimmer up through the loft opening. Two horses below nickered as they doubled their long legs under their bodies on the floor ... the sweet smell and burnt fried apples drifted up surrounding them all.

A nervous whiney snorted from below. Horses stomped their feet. Steve opened his eyes, smelled smoke ... his heart pounded. "Fire," he whispered, then yelled it as they both scrambled down the ladder and ran to unlock the two horse stalls. The horses neighed and snorted, pawed the ground, and ran out. Yellow tongues of flame lapped above the hot-plate like they could taste their own burning meal.

A gust of wind shot up glowing sparks like Roman Candles. Acrid smoke stung his nose and curled around. He grabbed the water hose and doused the burning wall. As it sizzled out, they both glanced at the main house. Did anyone see the fire? The collie came running.

"You've got to get out ... you can't be found here," he said.

Jane cast a dark shadow on the barn as she ran. Tears in her eyes reflected pinpoint glints of glow as she looked back.

The collie sniffed, and retreated back to the big house.

Steve worried about the reaction Gatsch would have to the fire. Fortunately Gatsch was pleased the horses got out OK and agreed it was an accident. Steve also thought about Jane ... his feelings for her were genuine now.

Two weeks later Milbur Vandos received a registered letter. It revealed that his true ancient great-grandfather, one he didn't even know about, had died a year ago back on Long Island. The letter from estate lawyers revealed Milbur was originally a grandson of one of the rich Vanderbilt family and the old man's will revealed how one Vanderbilt grandson had long ago, moved to California before World War I. He had gone broke and turned into the family black sheep, got arrested and to protect the family name, changed his name to Vandos.

Milbur received a belated $5,000 inheritance. A little Jiminy Cricket on his shoulder said, "Don't blow it at the track." He qualified himself for a Veteran's Home Loan, and for $2000 down bought a little house where his mom could live out in Lancaster on the desert edge near Andrews Air Force Base.

"Will you go for a ride in my new Mustang?" he asked Jane. "I'll show you the house I'm going to buy for my Mom. It's old but was a bargain."

They rolled to a stop along side the wire fence of the air force base. Other cars were lined up too. People stood along the fence looking upward. Steve jumped out and put the top down. The desert sun warmed their shoulders.

"Why are we stopping here?" Jane asked, as she put on sunglasses. "What are those people looking at?"

"Today is the 20th anniversary of the day the test pilot, Chuck Yeager, broke the sound barrier up there, and today two planes are going to do it just three seconds apart."

Just then ... BAAMMM ... BAAMMM ... the sky exploded two shotgun blasts -- quavering your ear drums in a prolonged double echoooo. People pointed up and cheered.

"I'm breaking a new barrier too," Steve exclaimed, "I've got a new job selling Fords. That's why I'm driving this Mustang, it's a loaner."

"Congratulations, that's earsplitting news"... she grinned searching upward.

Next week the Santa Anita grandstands hummed. Waves of voices crested again as the horses hurtled down the track. You strain to see through the flashing montage of jockey shirt colors. Jubilant screams charged with hope drown out the thundering hooves. It's not just a spectator sport. You empathize with horse and jockey ... you had studied the odds, post positions and track condition. You're up in the saddle. An electric roar in the grandstand ramps up your brain ... you strain forward in your seat ... you must win.

Early morning showers had turned the clay track into mud, more dangerous for both horse and rider. A damp smell hung in the air. Steve came up from the paddock and hung near the betting windows closest to Jane's box. Jane sauntered up, heads turned to follow her. She paused to check her Racing Form.

"I was hoping to see you here," he said, "Who do you like in this race?"

"I'm going with Mountain Morning, he won his last run in the mud," she looked up ... "And also I should tell you Steve, I'm not going to buy a horse."

"That's cool," he said, adding, "Where are you sitting?" He gambled.

Would she invite him to sit with her in public?

"Down in E Section near the finish line. I'm with Amanda my right hand girl, it's her birthday. I'm staking her today."

He waited, hoping -- her answer came.

"Come, join us. You'll remember her husband, my chauffer from Gatsch's front porch."

"Thank you." Blood surged in his temple.

The crowd's buzz rose to a fevered pitch as the 5th race thundered to a finish.   What beautiful horses. He helped her analyze the horses and odds ... the jockeys. They bet again ... she won -- hands in the air at the finish line.

"We're going up to the Crown Club afterwards. Can you join us?" she asked.His brain nearly exploded ... like he'd won the daily double -- up where just a few months ago they had insulted him.

Upstairs, Gatsch glared at them from across the room.

A week later Steve phoned her. She invited him to sit in her Santa Anita booth again. When he arrived at the track other people were sitting with her ... a mustached dude from Gatsch's studio. Steve shrunk back. The man got up and headed toward the betting windows.

Steve waited. *Will he return?* The guy didn't come back, so he joined Jane

"Sorry I'm late."

They studied the racing form.

"Who do you like," he asked.

She didn't answer, then said, "I'm selling my Beverly Hills home, and the studio wants me to play a new minor part with only a short speaking role.

"Ouch," he sympathized, thankful that she would confide in him.

"It will draw derision from the gossip columnists, but I'm glad to have it -- it's a gritty part and if I play it right, it'll gain attention."

"You can do it, Rosie. Just be yourself."

She lit a cigarette ... then dropped it and crushed it on the concrete with her foot.

"I hate smoking." She blew her last smoke-ring.

"I'm taking my name back to Vandos again," he said, "My new job selling

Fords is doing well." He hesitated. "I'm having a house warming party for my mom. Could you possibly come? ... I'll drive you out there."

"Yes, I'd be glad to, but I'll drive myself," she said graciously.

The desert heat sweltered the house as people nibbled little finger food nachos. Jane arrived followed by a big Dodge van. The van driver unloaded two window air-conditioning units as a house-cooling present. His mother cried and hugged Jane.

On the closing day of the summer racing season at Santa Anita, Steve and Rosie bantered. Her choice was a golden tan filly named 'Big Boogie.'

The odds were 10 to 1, but she had drawn a favorable number four post position and a top jockey.

"I like those odds," Steve said as they smiled and Hi-fived.

Rosie leaned over and whispered in his ear ..."Me too."

End

Christmas Episode

The Program Director, a mature cool guy, was never-the-less perturbed. Tall, jut-jawed and Clint Eastwood steely-eyed, he could persuade, cajole or bamboozle people as needed. He wore his work ethic like a badge of honor in the television production studio. And now the filming of this week's episode of the TV sit-com, "One Man's Family" had stalled. The malfunction caused by network executives changing the script again. Add that to rising tension from two days under the studio's 180 degree klieg lights which raised studio temperature as well as tempers among the cast and stage hands.

Now, the rehearsal for "One Man's Family" Christmas episode named "Best Ever Christmas" had been delayed again because writers had changed the scripts again.

The Director had patiently placated the actors ... soothing their easily bruised temperaments. However, now time had flown, leaving only its shadow behind. The deadline approached. The Director announced his edict.

"We only have time for a walk-through, to plan the shooting angles and complete the final shoot for tomorrow night's show," he proclaimed. That meant no time left for rehearsal to practice new lines, so cue cards would have to be relied on.

The Director scrutinized the big flat LCD screen monitor. He pointed fingers and yelled a heady mixture of orders.

Charles, the lead actor, who played the role of father, displayed panic on his pliable face.

"If I can just have the words in advance by Email," Charles said.

"My wife can read them into my computer. My computer can talk back and cue me. I'll learn my lines better."

"There's no time left," the Director said, "and cue cards are already made for all three cameras. We've got to shoot now.

The guys from the network are coming over to pick up the film in one hour."

Charles stared at the cue cards. Dialog lines were printed in different colors, green for Mama, and black for the teenage daughter and red for him, as the father character.

"I've g-got a problem," Charles stammered, his voice normally dramatic mellow, now crackled with falsetto fear.

"What are your demons, I'll drive them away." The Director smiled his 'trust me' face.

"I'm color blind," Charles blurted. "I need my lines in black, and I'm nervous about cue cards without a rehearsal."

The Director bit his lip and suppressed a feeling of spiders twitching in his blood ... the artery in his forehead bulged like a blue snake.

"The worst thing that can happen is that I call "Cut," the Director said, "and pretend we have technical problems, and you and I will go behind the set and figure everything out. I'm here for you Charles."

A few four-letter words later, the script guys and gals began re-lettering new cue cards for all three cameras. The Director walked the cast through each scene at each individual camera to make sure that no camera was ever in any other camera's shots or zooms.

He double checked again that no actor ever blocked any other actor's line of sight to their cue cards, now all with distinctly colored black readable block letters for Charles.

The shoot finally finished and the film reel of "Best Ever Christmas" rushed out the door on its way to the network.

As the Director exited the studio, the lash of frustration still laid on his back. It had been like being yoked to a plow of network red tape and megalomaniac writers and actors.

At his North Hollywood home that evening, the Director allowed himself to feel exhaustion. It hit him at the same time he realized his network boss hadn't called. Not a good sign. He asked his wife if he had any calls. His contract to direct the next six episodes had not been renewed even though he had inquired several times. He almost wished it wouldn't be renewed, then he wouldn't have to face all those prima donnas and bosses and un-nerving deadlines again. No more massaging over-inflated egos. *Is this job really important ... Is it worth it?*

He rose from the kitchen table, kissed his wife on top her head as he headed for his Lazy-boy chair to await the 7:30 prime-time slot. He turned on the TV and waited for the screen to flash on in full color. The theme music for "One Mans Family" came up. He had heard that syrupy tune a hundred times. Why didn't they change it? Nothing seemed right.

Just then his 6 year old son Timmy jumped up in his lap, hugged his neck and said.

"Let's watch your program Daddy."

End

Writers' Contests

There are many contests for writers to enter.

In the 'Fiction Story' genre, A Short Story is up to about 25,000 words, A Novel or Novella starts at about 60,000 words.

Below is the winner (not mine) of a contest for "The <u>worst</u> <u>first line</u> of a story."

The sun oozed over the horizon, shoved aside darkness, crept along the greensward, and, with sickly fingers, pushed through the castle window, revealing the pillaged princess, hand at throat, crown asunder, gaping in frenzied horror at the sated, sodden amphibian lying beside her, disbelieving the magnitude of the Frog's deception, screaming madly, "You lied!"

* * *

On the next page, you will find Fred Farris' story, *EXIT POLL*. This story won First Place Award in the Kansas Authors Club 2009 contest for 'Fiction less than 1000 words.'

Exit Poll

During the recent election, a voter decided to climb inside the new electronic voting machine to see what makes it work. Once inside its cavernous maze, he heard a strange crackling noise like the meshing of machinery in motion.

He followed the sound and entered a giant tunnel. Its curved walls were lined with fifty flashing lights, some red, some blue -- One for each state in the union. He came to a large courtyard. In its center were an elephant and a donkey. The animals were tethered together as a harnessed team. They marched in shuffling unison, circling around and around two huge millstones grinding grain between them in one common effort.

Curiosity overwhelmed the voter. He asked,

"Gentlemen, why are you two working together in such rare fashion?"

In unison they replied,

"Once every four years we join together to remind every voter of a famous wise man's words about the power of ONE person's vote."

"What words are those?" the voter asked.

The two beasts sat back on their haunches. Each held up a hoof. The elephant raised his right and the donkey his left. With one voice, they spoke.

"The wide world does not have the power I hold in one hand."

The voter nodded at their united wisdom. He turned and struggled back thru the labyrinth to its opening from where he had entered.

Once outside, a tall candidate garbed in red, white and blue stripes, wearing a top hat approached. The voter recognized him as a revered uncle.

"Who did you vote for?" his uncle asked.

"For you, Sam, for you."

"Thank you," Sam replied, "I worry that too many citizens vote against me these days by not voting at all, which is like 'Exiting' from the USA," he paused, then added,

"Remember, ask not for whom the poll tells ... it polls for thee!"

End

Thank You Captain

Back in the times when Trans World Airlines had its headquarters in Kansas City, flight 432 soared home through the night. Every seat was packed with people including the middle seat on my 3-seat side of the isle. A plumpish lady with a baby in a sling across her breast had squeezed into the middle seat making us tight-packed. I scrunched closer to the window.

The baby whined a crying gurgle for ten minutes which seemed longer ... then as its mother cuddled him and gave him a bottle, he finally cooed and fell asleep.

"What's the baby's name," I asked quietly.

"Heyse's de Jose" she said, "named after my father."

"Heysus, I repeated slowly as if misunderstanding.

"You would pronounce and spell it like Jesus," she said.

The plane droned on toward Kansas City as 10 PM approached. I stared out my little window. Sleet streaked horizontally outside the double plastic pane. I almost felt its cold splatter just four inches from my face as we plunged through the frozen dark. I could smell the cold ... as well as the baby.

Then, as if a gauze veil lifted outside, we came into a bright night. The clouds dissipated and scattered pinpoints of light salted the earth below.

Five minutes later, the captain's voice boomed from the overhead speakers.

"We are changing our flight path a little so you can see the Christmas lights on the Country Club Plaza – look out on the right side."

The dark night below blossomed into a blaze. Pinpoints of diamond and ruby glints ... ribbons of cranberry – oranges and greens flashed a kaleidoscope up at me. The quiet hum in the cabin muted into reverence and awe.

It reminded me of Christmas Eve at church when everyone held glowing candles in the dark. "All is calm, all is bright" ... I looked at the sleeping baby.

As we disembarked, the pilot's cockpit door cracked open. I flashed "thumbs up" and said, "Thank you Captain."

End

Steeple People*

A little boy clasped his hands together -- his two forefingers touched to form a tent-like pinnacle. He opened his hands up back-to-back ... interlocked fingers fumbling upward.

"Here's the church and here's the steeple, open the door, and here's all the people," he said, grinning up at his mom.

Kansas City's steeples are some of the metro's most salient beauty points, dozens of them sprinkled throughout the city pointing heavenward.

From the Church of the Immaculate Conception's golden dome downtown, to out in Lee's Summit where the towering glass of the Holy Spirit Catholic Church shines. From the twin shafts of nightlight probing the sky above Community Christian Church near the Plaza, to out on south Wornall Road where the white pinnacle on John Knox Presbyterian Kirk Church points upward. From northland's Gashland Baptist Church west to Asbury Methodist on 75th Street, to name just a few -- steeples adorn our neighborhoods like masts of schooners plowing though the ocean waves of life.

And the most dramatic of all.. the silver spiral soaring above the Community of Christ Church in Independence – an architectural magnificence surpassing all the spires of Europe.

For little boys and steeples, I love Kansas City.

End

* An essay as published in The Kansas City Star, "Reasons Why I Love Kansas City."
A feature article, 2009.

From Thomas Jefferson's 2nd Inaugural Address

Fellow citizens... When I contemplate our transcendent nation spread over wide and fruitful land, and engaged in commerce, traversing all the seas, I humble myself before its glory.

The opportunity to think freely and speak and write what we think, according to our Constitution and for the common good is our rare birthright. But every difference of opinion is not a difference of principal.

Whether we are Federalists or Democrats, all honest patriots. Let us then, with courage and confidence continue those principles, preserve our representative government and our striving to improve life and our great glorious nation and noble society.

.

Quiet Below

A Remembrance from WWII, by Sergeant Fred Farris.
Through the cold dusk the tall buildings of Boston's skyline looked like black silhouettes against a round mustard yellow background. That backdrop was the evening sun slowly setting, like a stage curtain going down to close the last act.

I strained to see through the mist; it was like breath on a mirror. Leaning on the deck rail of our troop ship, I stared at the fading skyline. A churning wake of white foam trailed out behind, rising and merging with the mist adding to the haziness of the scene. We all watched quietly.

"Do you think we'll ever see that skyline again?" my friend Ruiz said.

"I dunno," I answered barely above a whisper, wondering the same.

I recall now that as quiet as it was while I watched America fade in the distance, it was just a prelude to some much quieter moments just four days later.

We were the 86th Infantry Division -- 18,000 men and rifles and mortars and tanks and mine detectors and artillery -- all traveling in convoy of 19 ships painted in grey-green spotted camouflage. We were accompanied by four Navy destroyers and two sub-chasers on both flanks, escorting us across the cold North Atlantic.

German submarines still patrolled the Atlantic in November 1944. This late in the war, most of the large dangerous "Wolf Packs" of German U-boats had been destroyed or chased back to nearer their home bases, but the lure of attacking an important convoy still attracted the wolf out of his lair occasionally.

Our troopship was double-loaded, meaning 6,000 men, but with only 3,000 berths (actually hammocks) below deck. Therefore, to enable all troops to get equal sack time, the arrangement was that the 3,000 men below deck would trade places with the other 3,000 above deck; each 12 hour period. This rotation gave the guys below an opportunity to get up into fresh air which was welcomed by everyone. Down below it sometimes smelled bad because a few guys threw up from seasickness - and a greasy smell from the kitchen nearby.

I welcomed the 12 hour shifts topside, especially on clear nights. I lay on the metal deck looking up at the stars. Their pinpoints of lights slowly rotated in circles above, caused by our deck slowly undulating as the ship heaved through the ocean. I thought the moving heavens at night were fascinating, but the ship's slow rolling motion and stars revolving made some guys queasy ... but still better than down in the hold.

Below deck, sleeping was cramped and confined to your small personal cubicle of space sandwiched between hammocks swinging four-high, bunk bed style.

Between the rows of hammocks, access aisles about two feet wide felt as crowded as a sardine can. Guys jammed the aisles, talking, joking and generally buzzing like a bee hive.

However, one time we were all very quiet. We were below deck at the time. I heard a subdued Booomm, and felt a slight vibration. It wasn't loud, but a subdued deep tone. Then it came again, a low muffled Booomm, together with an immediate vibration like an echo. Ominous. Our chattering diminished dramatically. The quiet spread quickly from hull to hull. Every ear listened. Again Booomm, like a sledge hammer outside hitting against the steel hull next to your ear -- followed by a slight shuddering concussion on your ear drums – threatening danger.

After the first two or three booomms, we surmised that the external booooms were depth charges being dropped by our destroyer escort. We had been briefed about this possibility.

Booomm ... the dreaded reverberations came again ... like an echo from hell. The atmosphere turned tense. Were we being attacked by a sub??

"How come everyone's so quiet?" one guy asked.

"Be quiet and listen," a top sergeant said.

"It sounds like the voice of God," another said.

The booomms continued every 5 or 10 seconds for about three minutes. Waiting for the next one was as tense as waiting for a giant Grandfather clock to gong your doom. The silence between gongs stretched out ... in suspense ... then, after about ten loong minutes, the booms mercifully stopped.

Rumors ran that it was an attack, or at least a sub sighting. We never knew.

But we admitted among our selves we were scared in that strange quiet time where we acutely felt our helpless vulnerability.

Later, in combat conditions in Germany with all its noise and artillery explosions, I never complained once about the noise, remembering how really frightening total quiet can also be.

My buddy, Raymond Ruiz, was from New Orleans and part Cajun. His face, though swarthy and pock marked, usually beamed a friendly grin. His slight Cajun accent sounded almost like Brooklynese. His good natured bantering and humor, combined with being a husky, strong worker quickly marked him as a man you wanted on your team. This was important because we usually worked in two-man teams.

Our job, as signal corps linemen, was to run telephone lines from division headquarters forward to the three regimental command posts and even further forward to the combat Battalions. They all moved locations forward frequently with the advancing front lines. My "wire team," two men holding a big 70 pound spindle-reel of plastic–coated copper telephone wire between us, ran (rolled) the wire off the big spool and along the ground. Sometimes we needed to string the wire up in trees to prevent damage from tank tracks or incoming artillery explosions. When climbing trees, we wore telephone pole climbing spikes strapped to our legs.

We almost always needed two hands to work, so I carried my weapon, a 45 caliber sub-machine gun, slung over my shoulder. We called it a "burp-gun" because it belched short burps of bullets from its black snub-nosed barrel. Fortunately, I only had to use it once.

Ruiz and I were up in different trees spanning wire over a road when we heard two rifle shots like the pop-pop of distant fire crackers. A simultaneous shattering of a tree limb directly above my head told me a sniper was shooting at me.

While climbing down, we managed to spray a few staccato burp-burps in the general direction of the German rifleman. Luckily, we didn't need to pursue him because two of our infantry guys were nearby. They limped along the road toward the rear looking for the aid station. They turned and fired a few shots with their big Garand M1 rifles, driving the sniper away. Ruiz yelled, "thank, y'all," in his Cajun accent, and we continued running our wire reel out on the ground crouching as we ran. We also had truck mounted mobile radios, with 12 foot antennas ... but in the forward combat areas, radio wasn't used much because its transmission could be faulty and could also be intercepted by the enemy, so field telephones were relied on mostly.

Ruiz was a good soldier with real leadership qualities; confident, reliable, street smart, trustworthy. He was promoted to sergeant and later again jumped up again to 2nd Lieutenant at Officers' School. Years later, after the war, on a visit to New Orleans, my wife and I were shown around the inner recesses of the French Quarter by Major Ruiz, now commander of the New Orleans Police Department Vice Squad.

We never saw Boston again. Instead, we steamed back into New York harbor. Although we didn't know it at the time, we were the first full combat division to return to America after V-E (Victory in Europe) Day. It was June, 1945. Our troopship was greeted by a fleet of tugboats tooting their loud fog horns, even though it was a clear day. Then came a dozen motor boats, of all sizes loaded with people waving and escorting us past the beautiful Statue of Liberty. Those of us on deck wondered aloud ...

"Who are they waving at; must be some big-shot general arriving."

Then we saw some of the boat people holding up signs, "Welcome Home Boys!" and "Well Done 86th Infantry," and we waved back and yelled.

End

Ameriland

By Fred Farris

Come celebrate Ameriland
in fifty lands of marching bands
across five thousand miles.
Trumpet tunes with happy smiles.

From mid Missouriland to Maine
Oregoland, Michigaland, Pennsylvane
From California's redwood stands
To Florida's warming sands.

Kansaland, Alabam and Utah sing
rainbows over Colorado spring.
Ten thousand village voices blend
Illinois into Tennessee Smokey glen.

Texland and New York tall floors.
Georgia and Jersey shores.
East and West Virginia dine
with North and South Caroline.

Ameriland coast to coast.
United, strong enduring host. .
Watch over what she is and does.
Sing How Green My Valley Was.